THE POWER BOX

How Belief, Action, and Thought Transform Leaders and Build Legacies

By Lance Wardlaw

For permission requests, speaking engagements, or bulk orders, contact:

BAT Positive Press
Email: batpositive@gmail.com
Website: www.batpositive.com

Scripture quotations are from the King James Version of the Bible, which is in the public domain.

Published by BAT Positive Press,
Winston-Salem, North Carolina

ISBN: 979-8-9943172-0-4 (Paperback)
ISBN: 979-8-9943172-1-1 (Hardcover)
ISBN: 979-8-9943172-2-8 (eBook)

First Edition

Cover design by itztkhan
Interior design and formatting by itztkhan

Printed in the United States of America

TABLE OF CONTENTS

◆ ◆ ◆

The Power Box Promise

There's a green power box behind a playground in the Ellen C. Watson apartments on the west side of Spartanburg, South Carolina.

Most people wouldn't give it a second look. But for me, that power box represents one of the most defining moments of my life.

I was thirteen years old. I'd just been rejected—twice. My father said he didn't have room for me. My mother's boyfriend said the same. I felt unwanted. Forgotten. Like I didn't matter.

So I sat next to that power box and cried.

But somewhere in the middle of that breakdown, something shifted. I wiped my tears, looked up at the sky, and made a vow:

I'm going to be successful.

I'm going to prove them all wrong.

Nobody will ever make me feel this way again.

That promise changed my life.

Not because it was dramatic. Not because it was profound.

But because it became the fuel that pushed me through every hard season, every setback, every moment of doubt for the next three decades.

And it's the reason I'm writing this book.

This book exists because of a woman named Bobbie Higgins—my Aunt Bob.

When I was seven years old, my mother relinquished custody of me and my brother. Aunt Bob took us in. She didn't have to. She was already raising her two biological sons—Norman and Jammie—and had adopted our cousin Daniel, making it a total of five boys when she took us in. But she chose us anyway.

And in doing so, she gave me more than a home. She gave me a philosophy that would shape the rest of my life.

She called it simple. I call it life-changing.

> **"Be positive. Act positive. Think positive. And positive things will happen to you and for you."**

I heard those words thousands of times growing up. They became the soundtrack of my childhood. And over time, they became the operating system for how I navigated life, leadership, and legacy.

That philosophy—B.A.T. Positive—is what carried me from the housing projects of Spartanburg, South Carolina, to senior leadership in one of the most respected financial institutions in the country.

It's what helped me become the first African American Regional Lending Manager in the state of North Carolina within the Farm Credit System since the organization's founding in 1916.

It's what sustained me through nearly 20 years of leadership—the highs, the lows, the loneliness, and the breakthroughs.

And it's what I'm now teaching leaders, organizations, and individuals who want to unlock their potential and lead with impact.

What This Book Is About

This book is about three things:

1. **Belief** – Who you are at your core. Your values. Your character. Your anchor.

2. **Action** – What you do every single day. The discipline. The consistency. The sacrifice.

3. **Thought** – How you manage your mind. Your perspective. Your focus. Your resilience.

These three pillars—Belief, Action, and Thought—form the B.A.T. Positive framework.

And when you align all three, you don't just survive. You thrive.

You break cycles. You open doors. You build legacies.

Who This Book Is For

This book is for:

- **Emerging leaders** who are stepping into their first leadership roles and need a proven framework to guide them
- **Seasoned leaders** who are navigating new challenges and want to refine their approach
- **Aspiring leaders** who know they're capable of more but don't know how to unlock it

- **Anyone** who's ever felt overlooked, underestimated, or told they weren't enough

If you've ever felt like you were starting from behind, this book is for you.

If you've ever questioned whether you belong in the room, this book is for you.

If you've ever wondered how to lead with integrity, build positive teams, and create lasting impact, this book is for you.

What You'll Learn

In this book, you'll learn:

- How to anchor yourself in unshakable belief—even when circumstances try to rewrite your identity
- How to take consistent, disciplined action—even when motivation fades
- How to master your mindset—so your thoughts work for you, not against you
- How to lead through adversity, build positive cultures, and develop others
- How to navigate transitions, break cycles, and open doors for the next generation
- How to build a legacy that outlasts your career

But more than that, you'll see how B.A.T. Positive works in real life—because I'm going to show you.

You'll walk with me through my journey. You'll see the struggles, the breakthroughs, the mistakes, and the lessons learned. You'll see how B.A.T. carried me through moments when I didn't think I could keep going.

And you'll learn how to apply it in your own life.

A Note Before We Begin

This isn't a motivational book. This is a practical book.

I'm not here to hype you up. I'm here to equip you.

The principles in this book aren't theory. They're battle-tested. I've lived them. I've applied them. I've taught them. And I've seen them transform lives—including my own.

But here's the thing: **This only works if you do the work.**

Reading this book won't change your life. Applying it will.

So as you read, don't just consume. Engage. Reflect. Take the action challenges seriously. Do the hard work of examining your beliefs, your actions, and your thoughts.

Because that's where transformation happens.

Over thirty years ago, Aunt Bob looked at a broken kid from the projects and said, "Be positive. Act positive. Think positive."

She believed in me when I didn't believe in myself.

She saw potential in me that I couldn't see.

She planted a seed that would grow for decades.

And now, I'm passing that seed to you.

Your situation does not dictate your destination.

Your past does not define your future.

Your circumstances do not determine your destiny.

You do.

With belief. With action. With thought.

Now let's get to work.

PART 1: THE STORY

CHAPTER 1

The Projects, The Pain, and The Promise

Let me take you back to the beginning.

Not to the polished version of my story—the one that looks good on a resume or sounds inspiring from a stage.

I want to take you to the raw, unfiltered version. The one that shaped everything.

Because here's the truth: You can't fully understand where someone's going until you understand where they came from.

And I came from the projects.

Tobias Hartwell: Ages 0-7

I was born in Spartanburg, South Carolina, and for the first seven years of my life, I lived in a place called Tobias Hartwell.

It was the projects—subsidized housing for low-income families in Spartanburg, South Carolina.

My mother did her best. She loved us. But life was hard, and she was young, and she was doing everything she could just to survive.

Our home wasn't stable. It wasn't because my mother didn't care—it was because stability was a luxury we couldn't afford.

There was a constant flow of people in and out of our lives. Uncles. Great uncles. Boyfriend. Significant others. People who stayed for a season and then disappeared.

And with every new person came new rules, new tensions, new instability.

I learned early that home wasn't always a safe place. Sometimes it was loud. Sometimes it was chaotic. Sometimes it was better to be invisible.

So I became very good at being invisible.

I have a memory from those years that I've never forgotten.

I was hiding in a closet.

I don't remember why. I don't remember who I was hiding from. But I remember the feeling.

The feeling of wanting to disappear. The feeling of not being safe. The feeling of not knowing what would happen next.

That's what instability does to a child. It teaches you to brace for impact. To expect disappointment. To protect yourself.

But it also planted something in me—a hunger for something different. A belief that life didn't have to be this way.

I just didn't know how to get there yet.

The Woman Who Changed Everything: Aunt Bob

When I was seven years old, everything changed.

My mother made one of the hardest decisions a parent can make: she relinquished custody of me and my brother, Lester.

She knew she couldn't give us the stability we needed. She knew we deserved more than she could provide in that season of her life.

And so she called her sister—my Aunt Bob.

Aunt Bob's full name is Bobbie Ann Higgins, but everyone called her Aunt Bob. She was my mother's sister, and she was the kind of woman who didn't just talk about doing the right thing—she did it.

Aunt Bob already had her hands full. She was raising two biological sons—Norman and Jammie. She'd also taken in our cousin Daniel, who she treated as her own.

That made three boys already.

And then she said yes to two more.

She didn't have to. She could have said, "I'm sorry, but I can't." And no one would have blamed her.

But that's not who Aunt Bob was.

She believed that family takes care of family. That children deserve stability. That love isn't just a feeling—it's a commitment.

So she took us in. And in doing so, she saved my life.

A New Home: The Eastside

We moved into Aunt Bob's apartment on the Eastside of Spartanburg.

It wasn't the projects. It was a middle-class apartment complex. Clean. Quiet. Safe.

For the first time in my life, I felt like I could breathe.

Now there were five boys in the house: me, my brother Lester, our cousin Daniel, and Aunt Bob's two sons, Norman and Jammie.

It was crowded. It was loud. But it was stable.

And that made all the difference.

Aunt Bob ran a tight ship. She had rules. Structure. Expectations.

And she had a philosophy that she repeated to us constantly:

> **"Be positive. Act positive. Think positive. And positive things will happen to you and for you."**

At the time, I didn't fully understand what that meant. I just knew that Aunt Bob believed in something bigger than our circumstances.

She believed we could be more. Do more. Become more.

And because she believed it, I started to believe it too.

Aunt Bob's Three Core Rules

Aunt Bob had three non-negotiable rules in her house:

1. Respect

"You will respect me, you will respect this house, and you will respect each other."

Disrespect wasn't tolerated. Not toward her. Not toward each other. Not toward anyone.

She taught us that respect was the foundation of everything. If you can't respect people, you can't build relationships. And if you can't build relationships, you can't build a life.

2. Work Hard

"Nothing in this world is free. You earn what you get."

Aunt Bob worked minimum-wage jobs to provide for us. She worked long hours. She sacrificed constantly.

And she expected us to do the same.

We had chores. We had responsibilities. We had to contribute.

She didn't believe in entitlement. She believed in effort.

3. Be Positive

"Be positive. Act positive. Think positive."

This wasn't just a saying. It was a way of life.

Even when things were hard—and they often were—Aunt Bob chose to see the good. She chose to believe things could get better. She chose to focus on what was possible instead of what was broken.

And she taught us to do the same.

The Lesson of Service

One of the most powerful lessons Aunt Bob taught us was the importance of service.

Every year during the Christmas season, Aunt Bob would take us to a nursing home to visit the residents.

We'd bring small gifts—nothing expensive, just tokens of care. We'd spend time with people who were often forgotten by the world.

And Aunt Bob would remind us: "We don't have much. But we can always give something."

That lesson stuck with me.

Service isn't about what you have. It's about what you give.

You don't have to be rich to make a difference. You don't have to be powerful to have impact. You just have to show up and serve.

That lesson would shape my entire leadership philosophy decades later.

Faith as the Foundation

Aunt Bob was a woman of deep faith. And she made sure that faith was woven into the fabric of our home.

Every morning started with prayer.

Every meal ended with grace.

Every Sunday, we were in church.

And when life got hard, Aunt Bob would quote Philippians 4:13:

She didn't just say it. She lived it.

And because she lived it, we believed it.

Faith became the anchor that held us steady when everything else was shaking.

I Was Becoming Lance

Living with Aunt Bob didn't erase the pain of my early years. But it gave me something I'd never had before: stability.

For the first time, I knew what to expect. I knew the rules. I knew I was safe. I knew I was wanted.

And in that stability, something began to grow.

Belief.

Belief that I could be more than my circumstances.

Belief that I could do hard things.

Belief that my past didn't have to define my future.

I was becoming Lance.

Not the scared kid from Tobias Hartwell. Not the kid who hid in closets.

But the Lance who would one day lead teams, break barriers, and build programs that changed lives.

That transformation didn't happen overnight. But it started in Aunt Bob's home.

Age Thirteen: The Crisis

But before I tell you about high school and college, I need to take you back to a moment that almost broke me.

Because stability doesn't last forever. And when you're thirteen years old, the world can change in an instant.

Aunt Bob was struggling. Her oldest son was going through a difficult season, and she needed to focus on her two birth sons. She loved me and my brother, but she couldn't do it all anymore.

She needed to realign her household.

My brother Lester went to live with our youngest aunt, Aunt Von.

And Aunt Bob reached out to my father to see if he would take me in.

He told her he needed a day to think about it. To discuss it with his wife.

For one day, I let myself hope.

I let myself believe that maybe, finally, my father wanted me. That maybe I'd have a place where I truly belonged.

But the next day, he said no.

He had a three-bedroom home. A spare bedroom. My sister lived there.

But there was no room for me.

Years later, I would learn the truth: my father didn't think I was his child.

After my father's rejection, Aunt Bob called my mother. She agreed to take me in.

But her boyfriend—the man she was living with, the father of my baby brother—said no too.

Two rejections. Two men who had space but chose not to make room.

Ellen C. Watson: The Summer of Waiting

With nowhere else to go, I was sent to stay with my oldest aunt—Aunt Daisey (also known as Aunt Tootsie)—in the Ellen C. Watson apartments.

The projects.

The agreement was that I could stay if my mother came too. And at first, she did. But then she left. She went back to her boyfriend. Back to her life.

And I was left alone.

Aunt Tootsie was kind, but she had her own life. I wasn't her responsibility, and we both knew it.

The days were long. The nights were short.

I had no friends there. Nothing to do.

The playground became my refuge.

I'd sit on the swings and watch the cars go by, hoping—desperately hoping—that one of them would be Aunt Bob's car. That she'd come back for me.

But day after day, she didn't come.

The Power Box Moment

One afternoon, I got tired of swinging. Tired of watching. Tired of waiting.

I sat down next to a green power box behind the playground.

Back on the Eastside, my friends and I used to huddle around a power box just like this one after playing football. We'd sit there and talk, joke, dream.

But this time, I was alone.

And I wasn't dreaming.

I was drowning.

Sitting there, everything hit me at once.

My father didn't want me.

My mother's boyfriend didn't want me.

My mother had left—again.

Aunt Bob hadn't come back.

I felt forgotten. Unwanted. Like I didn't matter.

Even though I had a roof over my head, **I felt homeless.**

So I cried.

I cried harder than I'd ever cried in my life.

But somewhere in the middle of that breakdown, something shifted.

I wiped my tears. I looked up at the sky. And I made a vow:

I'm going to be successful.

I'm going to prove them all wrong.

Nobody will ever make me feel this way again.

That promise became my North Star.

It became the fuel that pushed me through every hard season, every setback, every moment of doubt.

And decades later, I can look back and say: **I kept the promise.**

Not perfectly. Not without struggle. But I kept it.

The Return

Weeks later, Aunt Bob came back for me.

She'd sought counsel from Norma Sue Pitts—a woman who was like a mother and mentor to her. And after that conversation, Aunt Bob made the decision: she was coming back.

When I saw her pull up, I felt overwhelming relief.

Joy. Gratitude. Safety.

I was going home.

Not to my mother. Not to my father. But to the woman who had chosen me—again.

Aunt Bob didn't have to come back for me. She had every reason not to.

But she did.

And that made all the difference.

Why This Story Matters

Let me be clear about something: This isn't a sob story.

This is a story about cycles—and how they can be broken.

This is a story about belief—and how one person's belief can change the trajectory of another person's life.

This is a story about resilience—and how pain can become purpose if you choose to let it.

Your zip code doesn't determine your destiny.

Your starting point doesn't dictate your ending point.

Your past doesn't define your future.

I'm proof of that.

And if I can do it, so can you.

Reflection Questions

Before you move to the next chapter, take a moment to reflect:

1. **What cycles are you breaking?** What patterns from your past are you choosing not to repeat?
2. **Who believed in you when you didn't believe in yourself?** Who was your Aunt Bob?
3. **What's your power box moment?** When did you make a promise to yourself that changed everything?

1. **Write down one cycle you're committed to breaking.** It could be in your family, your leadership, your community. Name it. Own it.

2. **Reach out to someone who believed in you.** Thank them. Let them know the impact they had on your life.

3. **Make a promise to yourself.** What vow are you making today that will fuel you through the next decade?

CHAPTER 2

Becoming Lance

This chapter is called "Becoming Lance" for a reason.

Because the Lance you met in Chapter 1—the kid from the projects, the one nobody wanted—that's not the Lance who would eventually lead teams, break barriers, and build programs that changed lives.

Something had to happen between that kid and that leader.

And that something was B.A.T. Positive—lived out in real time, in real situations, long before I even understood what I was doing.

This chapter is about that transformation. About the models I found. The moments that tested me. The choices I made.

This is the story of how a philosophy became a framework. And how a framework became a life.

High School: Finding My Identity

By the time I reached high school, I was no longer the scared kid hiding in closets or sitting alone by power boxes.

I had become someone different. Someone stronger. Someone with a little more confidence.

But I still didn't know who I was.

I was searching for identity. Trying to figure out where I fit. Trying to understand what kind of man I was going to become.

And like most teenagers, I found my identity in two places: sports and peers.

Football and the Lessons of Discipline

I played football at Spartanburg High School under the legendary Coach Doc Davis. I wasn't the most talented player on the field, but I was disciplined. I showed up. I worked hard. I did what the coaches asked me to do.

Our rivalry games were intense—the kind where the entire community showed up and the stakes felt higher than just a scoreboard.

Football taught me about teamwork, sacrifice, and pushing through pain. It taught me that talent alone wasn't enough—you had to be willing to put in the work.

But more than that, football gave me structure. Practices. Games. Playbooks. Expectations. It was the kind of structure Aunt Bob had been building in me at home, now reinforced on the field.

I was learning what it meant to be part of something bigger than myself.

The Influence of Peers

But high school wasn't just about sports. It was also about navigating peer pressure and figuring out who I wanted to be.

I had friends who were testing boundaries in dangerous ways. Some were experimenting with drugs. Others were causing trouble—petty theft, vandalism, the kind of rebellion that felt exciting in the moment but had real consequences. And of course, there was the typical teenage exploration of relationships and sex.

I could have easily followed them. The pull was there. The environment I came from made it easy to justify. And honestly, there were moments when I tested those boundaries myself.

But Aunt Bob's voice was always in my head: *Be positive. Act positive. Think positive.*

I had to make a choice: Would I follow the crowd into decisions I'd regret, or would I follow the path Aunt Bob had laid out for me?

I chose the path.

Not perfectly. Not without mistakes. But I chose it.

And that choice—made over and over again in small moments—shaped the trajectory of my life.

B.A.T. Reflection:

Looking back, I can see B.A.T. forming in me even then:

Belief: I believed I could be different. I believed I didn't have to follow the crowd just because it was easier.

Action: I chose to stay on the field, stay in school, stay focused on the future Aunt Bob said was possible.

Thought: I focused on what I could become, not on what I was tempted to do. I kept my mind on the goal.

I didn't have the language for it yet. But the philosophy was taking root.

The First In-Person Model: My Brother Lester

Before any coach, before any mentor, there was Lester.

My older brother, Lester Wardlaw, was my first hero.

He was the one who showed me what was possible. He was the one who challenged me to think beyond my current circumstances. He was the one who paved the way for me to follow.

Lester had a positive attitude that was infectious. Even when things were hard—and they were often hard—he found a way to keep moving forward. He took risks. He believed in himself. He refused to let our environment define him.

And because he led the way, I had a path to follow.

When I didn't know what to do, I watched Lester. When I didn't know if something was possible, I looked at what Lester had already done. When I felt like giving up, I remembered that Lester never quit.

He set the bar high. And he made me believe I could reach it.

Lester wasn't perfect—none of us are. But he was consistent. He was intentional. He was determined. And he showed me, through his actions, that we didn't have to be products of our environment. We could be architects of our future.

To this day, Lester remains one of the most influential people in my life. Not because he had all the answers, but because he was willing to go first. To take the risks. To show me that a different life was possible.

B.A.T. Reflection:

Here's how Lester modeled B.A.T. for me:

Belief: He believed we could rise above our circumstances. That belief became contagious.

Action: He didn't just talk about change—he lived it. He made moves. He took chances. He showed me what action looked like.

Thought: His positive attitude, even in hard times, taught me that mindset matters. How you think about your situation shapes how you navigate it.

Lester was my first in-person model. And he remains my hero.

The Power of Models: Jerry Rice

One of the most influential figures in my high school years wasn't someone I knew personally. It was someone I watched on TV every Sunday: Jerry Rice.

Jerry Rice wasn't just a football player. He was a model of excellence.

I studied him. I watched how he ran routes. How he caught passes. How he trained. How he carried himself.

But more than that, I watched his work ethic.

Jerry Rice was famous for his off-season training regimen. He would run hills in the scorching heat. He would do drills that other players wouldn't touch. He worked harder than everyone else—not because he had to, but because he chose to.

And that taught me something critical: **Talent is a starting point. Work ethic is what separates the good from the great.**

I wasn't the most talented player on my team. But I could control my effort. I could control my discipline. I could control how hard I worked.

So I did.

I trained like Jerry Rice trained. I pushed myself the way he pushed himself. And while I never became a professional athlete, I learned a lesson that would carry me through my entire career:

Excellence isn't about being the best. It's about giving your best—every single day.

B.A.T. Reflection:

Here's how B.A.T. showed up in my admiration for Jerry Rice:

Belief: I believed I could be excellent if I worked harder than everyone else.

Action: I studied Jerry Rice's every move and applied it to my own training.

Thought: I focused on what was possible, not on what I lacked. I refused to let my circumstances limit my effort.

Coach Smiley: Focus and Belief

In addition to football, I ran track and field. And that's where I met Coach Smiley.

Coach Smiley was different from any coach I'd had before. He wasn't just concerned with times and technique. He was concerned with who we were becoming.

He taught me two things that would stay with me forever: **focus and belief.**

Focus: Coach Smiley would tell us, "If you don't focus on the finish line, you'll never get there. Distractions will always be there. Your job is to stay locked in on what matters."

That lesson extended far beyond the track. It became a principle for life. Focus on the goal. Block out the noise. Stay disciplined.

Belief: He also taught me that belief wasn't just about confidence—it was about commitment. "You have to believe you can do it," he'd say, "but belief without work is just wishful thinking."

He pushed me. He challenged me. He refused to let me settle for mediocrity.

And because he believed in me, I started to believe in myself.

Though Coach Smiley is no longer with us, his impact on my life remains. He planted seeds that would grow for decades. He showed me that one person's belief can change the trajectory of another person's life.

I honor his memory. And I carry his lessons with me always.

B.A.T. Reflection:

Coach Smiley modeled the power of focus and belief:

Belief: He believed in me when I didn't fully believe in myself. That belief became a mirror I could see myself in differently.

Action: He didn't just talk about potential—he invested time in developing it. He coached me, mentored me, pushed me.

Thought: He challenged me to think bigger. To see beyond my circumstances. To focus on what I could become, not what I'd been.

That's the power of a model. That's the power of someone who sees you and speaks life into you.

College: East Tennessee State University

After high school, I enrolled at East Tennessee State University (ETSU) in Johnson City, Tennessee, where I pursued a degree in Finance and Banking.

ETSU wasn't a historically Black university. It was a predominantly white institution, and I was stepping into an environment very different from what I'd known growing up.

But I was ready. Or at least, I thought I was.

The reality of college hit quickly: **I was broke.**

Aunt Bob had done everything she could to help me get there, but there was no financial safety net. I had to figure out how to survive on my own.

The Office of Multicultural Affairs

One of the best decisions I made in college was taking a job with the Office of Multicultural Affairs at ETSU.

That job changed me.

It wasn't just about the paycheck—though the funding I received helped me cover basic needs like food and supplies. It was about what I learned.

Working in Multicultural Affairs exposed me to people from different backgrounds, cultures, and perspectives. I learned how to navigate diverse spaces. I learned how to listen. I learned how to build bridges between people who didn't naturally understand each other.

I learned about people.

And that education—the kind you don't get in a classroom—would serve me for the rest of my career.

The Support System That Kept Me Going

But I didn't do college alone.

My mother chipped in when she could. My father helped from time to time. And Aunt Bob—always Aunt Bob—did everything in her power to make sure I had what I needed.

And then there was Jammie.

Jammie and I made the hour and forty-five-minute drive from Spartanburg to Johnson City countless times over those four years. Aunt Bob made sure we had transportation. She sacrificed to secure travel for us, even when money was tight.

That drive became a lifeline. It connected me to home, to family, to the people who believed in me.

I didn't make it through college on my own. I made it because people invested in me.

The Struggle to Stay Afloat

Even with support, college was hard.

There were nights when I wasn't sure I'd have enough money for the next week. There were moments when I wondered if I was cut out for this. There were times when quitting felt easier than continuing.

I remember calling Aunt Bob during one particularly hard season and telling her I didn't think I could do it. I was exhausted. I was overwhelmed. I was ready to quit.

And you know what she said?

"Lance, you can do all things through Christ who strengthens you. You've come too far to quit now."

That was it. No long pep talk. No promises that it would get easier.

Just a reminder of what she'd been teaching me my whole life: **You have what it takes. Now act like it.**

So I kept going.

I worked. I studied. I pushed through the exhaustion.

And eventually, I graduated from East Tennessee State University with a degree in Finance and Banking.

Not with honors. Not at the top of my class.

But I finished.

And that was enough.

B.A.T. Reflection:

College was where B.A.T. became a survival strategy:

Belief: I had to believe I could finish, even when everything in me wanted to quit.

Action: I showed up every day. I worked through Multicultural Affairs. I leaned on my support system. I didn't let exhaustion be an excuse.

Thought: I focused on the finish line, not the struggle. I reminded myself daily: "This is temporary. Keep going."

B.A.T. wasn't just philosophy anymore. It was how I survived.

The Man I Was Becoming

By the time I graduated, I had grown from the uncertain teenager I once was into someone who believed he could succeed.

I had become someone different.

I had learned what it meant to work hard. To push through adversity. To believe in myself even when others didn't.

I had learned from models like Jerry Rice and Coach Smiley what excellence, focus, and belief looked like.

I had been shaped by my brother Lester, who showed me that rising above circumstances was possible.

I had navigated a predominantly white institution and learned how to build bridges across differences.

I had survived moments that should have broken me—poverty, rejection, exhaustion—and come out stronger.

I was becoming the man I'd promised myself I would be.

And the journey was just beginning.

But here's what I need you to understand:

Belief, action, and thought weren't just helping me. They were becoming my operating system.

And in the next three chapters, I'm going to break down each pillar—so you can build this same operating system in your own life.

First, let's talk about Belief. Because without a strong foundation, nothing else matters.

Reflection Questions

Before you move to the next chapter, take a moment to reflect:

1. **Who were your models?** Who did you look up to growing up? What did they teach you about excellence, discipline, or character?
2. **What was your "power box moment"?** When did you make a promise to yourself that changed your trajectory?
3. **How has B.A.T. shown up in your life**—even if you didn't have language for it? Where have you seen belief, action, and thought align to carry you through hard times?

Action Challenges

1. **Write down your power box promise.** What commitment are you making to yourself today? What will you not compromise on?
2. **Identify one model in your life.** Someone who exemplifies excellence, character, or discipline. Study them. Learn from them. Apply what you observe.
3. **Share your story with someone younger than you.** Your journey—your struggles, your breakthroughs—could be exactly what someone else needs to hear.

PART 2: THE FRAMEWORK

CHAPTER 3

Believe It: The Power of Belief

If you've made it this far, you know my story.

You've met Aunt Bob. You've walked with me through the projects of Spartanburg. You've seen how B.A.T. Positive was planted in me long before I understood what it was.

Now it's time to break down the framework.

Over the next three chapters, I'm going to show you how to apply B.A.T. Positive in your own life—not as theory, but as a practical operating system that transforms how you lead, how you live, and how you impact others.

We're starting with the foundation: Belief.

Because here's the truth: **If your belief system is broken, nothing else matters.**

You can take all the action in the world, but if you don't believe you're capable, you'll sabotage yourself.

You can think positive thoughts all day long, but if your core beliefs are rooted in fear, shame, or limitation, those thoughts won't stick.

Belief is the anchor. It's the foundation. It's where transformation begins.

So let's talk about what it means to *be* positive.

What "Be Positive" Really Means

When Aunt Bob said "be positive," she wasn't asking me to pretend everything was fine.

She wasn't telling me to ignore my circumstances or suppress my emotions.

She was teaching me about identity.

Be positive is about **who you are at your core**—your values, your character, your integrity, your faith.

It's about anchoring yourself in something solid so that when life shakes you (and it will), you don't crumble.

Think of it this way:

Action is what you *do*.
Thought is how you *think*.
Belief is who you *are*.

And who you are determines everything else.

The Three Foundations of Belief

When I talk about belief, I'm talking about three foundational elements:

1. **Values** – What you stand for
2. **Character** – Who you are when nobody's watching
3. **Faith** – What anchors you when everything else fails

Let's break each one down.

Foundation 1: Values - What You Stand For

Your values are your non-negotiables. They're the principles you won't compromise on, even when it costs you.

For me, Aunt Bob instilled values early:

Integrity – Don't lie. Ever. "I can handle anything but dishonesty," she'd say.

Family – Always have your brothers' backs. You're all you've got.

Hard work – Nothing worth having comes easy. You earn what you get.

Service – Use what you have to help others. Even when you don't have much.

Faith – God is your anchor. When everything else fails, He won't.

These weren't just words on a wall. These were lived principles. And they became the filter through which I made every major decision in my life.

Here's why values matter:

When you don't know what you stand for, you'll fall for anything.

When you don't have clearly defined values, you'll make decisions based on convenience, comfort, or peer pressure—and you'll regret it later.

But when your values are clear, decision-making becomes simpler. Not easier, but clearer.

The $100 Fee That Defined My Character

Let me tell you about a moment when character cost me—literally.

I was working on a real estate purchase for a couple who lived a few states away. They were detail-oriented—the kind of customers who paid close attention to every number, every document, every deadline.

They'd been communicating with me closely throughout the entire loan process. We'd gotten all the conditions fulfilled. Everything was on track.

They were traveling by car to North Carolina—a week-long trip—and they'd already prepared their cashier's check based on the closing costs I'd given them.

Then, as we were preparing the final fees and legal instructions, the processor identified a problem.

We'd missed a critical fee. A $100 fee that I'd overlooked.

It was an honest mistake. But it was my mistake.

I had two choices:

Choice 1: Call the customers and explain. Ask them to bring an additional $100 to closing.

Legally, that was fine. It was a legitimate fee. They'd understand.

Choice 2: " Eat the fee " — which is lender language for covering or waiving the fee.

Here's what made it complicated:

They were already on the road. They'd already prepared their check. Asking them to bring more money at the last minute would create stress, inconvenience, and potentially damage my reputation—and the company's.

So I made the decision: I would "eat the fee."

I called the customers and explained what happened. I apologized for the oversight and assured them we'd handle it.

Here's what could have happened if I'd made the other choice:

They show up to closing expecting one number—and get hit with an unexpected $100. They're frustrated. They question my competence. They tell other people about their experience. My reputation takes a hit. The company's reputation takes a hit.

All because I tried to save $100.

But here's what actually happened:

The closing went smoothly. The customers were grateful for the transparency. They referred multiple people to me over the years.

And I learned something critical: **Your reputation is built in moments when integrity costs you something.**

Anyone can do the right thing when it's convenient. Character is doing the right thing when it's not.

That $100 turned out to be one of the wisest decisions I made during that season of my life.

Defining Your Values

So here's the question: **What are your values?**

Not the values you *think* you should have. Not the values that sound good on paper.

The values you actually live by.

Here's how to identify them:

1. Look at your decisions.
What do you consistently choose, even when it's hard? That's a value.

2. Look at what makes you angry.
When you see someone violate a principle and it stirs something deep in you, that's probably a value you hold.

3. Look at what you won't compromise on.
Even when it costs you—money, relationships, opportunities—what do you refuse to bend on? That's a core value.

A Simple Exercise to Identify Your Core Values

Here's a practical exercise I use with leaders:

Step 1: Think of a moment when you felt most alive, most fulfilled, most "you."
What were you doing? Who were you with? What made it meaningful?

Step 2: Think of a moment when you felt angry, frustrated, or deeply disappointed.
What value was violated? What principle was crossed?

Step 3: Look at your last three major decisions.
What did you say "yes" to? What did you say "no" to? What patterns emerge?

Step 4: If you could only be remembered for three things, what would they be?
That's a clue to your deepest values.

Write down what emerges. Don't edit. Don't overthink. Just capture what's true.

Then narrow it to your top 5 values and write them somewhere you'll see them daily.

Once you identify your values, **write them down.**

Make them visible. Put them on your wall. Reference them when you're making hard decisions.

Because when life gets complicated—and it will—your values will be the compass that guides you home.

Foundation 2: Character - Who You Are When Nobody's Watching

Values are what you stand for. Character is who you are when it doesn't benefit you to be that person.

Character is integrity in the dark.

It's doing the right thing when no one will know if you don't.

It's keeping your word even when breaking it would be easier.

It's treating people with respect even when they can't do anything for you.

Aunt Bob taught me character through her actions, not her words.

She could have cut corners. She could have taken shortcuts. She could have compromised to make life easier.

But she didn't.

She worked minimum-wage jobs with dignity. She paid her debts, even when it took years. She kept her promises to us, even when it cost her.

And we watched.

Kids don't do what you say. They do what you do. And what Aunt Bob *did* was show us what character looked like.

Character Is Built in Small Moments

Here's what most people don't understand about character: **It's not built in the big moments. It's built in the small ones.**

It's built when you:

- Tell the truth even though lying would be easier
- Keep your commitment even though you're exhausted
- Treat the janitor with the same respect you treat the CEO
- Do your job well even though nobody's watching
- Admit your mistake even though you could hide it

Those small moments compound.

And over time, they create a reputation. They build trust. They make you someone people want to follow.

Here's the test:

If someone followed you around with a camera for a week—not just at work, but at home, in traffic, when you're frustrated, when you're tired—

would they see consistency between who you say you are and who you actually are?

If the answer is no, you have character work to do.

And that's okay. We all do. Character is built over a lifetime, not in a moment.

But you have to be intentional about it.

Foundation 3:
Faith - What Anchors You When Everything Else Fails

The third foundation of belief is faith.

For me, faith is rooted in God. It's anchored in Scripture. It's the belief that **I can do all things through Christ who strengthens me** (Philippians 4:13).

But here's what I want you to understand: **Faith isn't just religious. It's foundational.**

Even if you don't share my specific faith, you need *something* that anchors you when life falls apart.

You need something bigger than yourself to hold onto when everything else is shaking.

For some people, it's a deep belief in purpose—that they're here for a reason and that their life has meaning beyond themselves.

For others, it's a commitment to a cause—something they're willing to fight for even when it's hard.

For me, it's God.

Faith Carried Me Through

There were moments in my life when faith was the *only* thing that kept me going.

When I was thirteen years old, sitting next to that power box at Ellen C. Watson—it was faith that whispered, *You're not forgotten. You're not unwanted. You have a purpose.*

When I was in college, broke and exhausted, ready to quit—it was Aunt Bob's reminder of Philippians 4:13 that pulled me through.

When I stepped into senior leadership and felt the weight of being "the first"—when I questioned if I belonged, if I was good enough—it was faith that steadied me.

Faith doesn't eliminate the struggle. But it gives you an anchor in the storm.

When My Belief Was Tested: The Weight of Being "The First"

Let me tell you about a moment when my belief system was under attack.

It was 2021. I'd just been promoted to Regional Lending Manager—the first African American in North Carolina within the Farm Credit System to reach that level since 1916.

I should have been celebrating. But instead, I was questioning everything.

Am I really qualified for this?
Did they promote me because I'm capable—or to check a diversity box?
What if I fail? What if I prove the doubters right?

The weight of being "the first" felt crushing. Every decision felt magnified. Every mistake felt like it could reinforce negative stereotypes.

I remember sitting in my office one night, looking at the leadership org chart with my name on it, and thinking: *Maybe I don't belong here.*

That's when I had to anchor back to my belief system.

I asked myself the questions I'm asking you now:

- What do I know to be true about who I am—regardless of what anyone else thinks?
- What are my core values? Have they changed just because the title changed?
- Do I believe God equipped me for this role—or do I believe the doubters?

I chose to believe:

- I earned this position through years of consistent excellence
- My character and competence qualified me, not my race
- Being "the first" wasn't a burden—it was an opportunity to open doors for others

That belief shift changed everything.

Instead of shrinking under the weight, I stood taller. Instead of playing it safe, I led boldly. Instead of worrying about what people thought, I focused on serving my team and delivering results.

And here's what I learned: Your belief system will be tested—especially when you step into new levels of leadership.

The question isn't *if* your belief will be attacked. It's *how you'll respond when it is.*

What's Your Anchor?

So here's my question for you: **What anchors you?**

When life gets hard—and it will—what do you hold onto?

When you're facing rejection, failure, loss, or uncertainty—what keeps you from giving up?

If you don't have an answer to that question, you need to find one.

Because belief without an anchor is just wishful thinking. It's motivation that fades when things get hard.

But belief *with* an anchor? That's unshakable.

The Enemies of Belief

Now that we've talked about what builds belief, let's talk about what destroys it.

Because here's the reality: **Your belief system is under attack every single day.**

There are forces—internal and external—working to tear down what you're trying to build.

Here are the three biggest enemies of belief:

Enemy 1: Comparison

Comparison is the thief of belief.

When you measure your progress against someone else's highlight reel, you'll always feel like you're falling short.

When you look at where someone else is and forget how far *you've* come, you'll start to believe you're not good enough.

Comparison makes you focus on what you lack instead of what you have.

And that erodes belief faster than almost anything else.

Here's the antidote:

Stop comparing your beginning to someone else's middle.

Stop measuring your Chapter 2 against someone else's Chapter 10.

Your journey is your own. Your timeline is your own. Your purpose is your own.

Run your race. Not theirs.

Enemy 2: Past Failures

Your past does not define your future.

But if you let it, your past will convince you that you're not capable of more.

Every failure, every mistake, every moment you fell short—if you replay those moments on repeat, they'll become your identity.

You'll start to believe: "I'm the kind of person who fails. I'm the kind of person who doesn't follow through. I'm the kind of person who's not good enough."

And once you believe that, it becomes a self-fulfilling prophecy.

Here's the truth:

Your past is data, not destiny.

Your mistakes are lessons, not life sentences.

Your failures are feedback, not final verdicts.

Learn from them. Don't live in them.

Enemy 3: Negative Voices

The third enemy of belief is the voices that tell you you're not enough.

Maybe it's a parent who never believed in you.

Maybe it's a coach who told you you'd never make it.

Maybe it's a boss who said you didn't have what it takes.

Maybe it's a friend who doubted you.

Or maybe—most dangerously—it's *your own voice* telling you you're not capable.

Those voices are loud. And if you listen to them long enough, you'll start to believe them.

Here's what you have to understand:

Not every voice deserves a seat at your table.

Some voices need to be muted. Some need to be removed. Some need to be replaced.

And the way you do that is by surrounding yourself with voices that *build* you instead of *breaking* you.

Building an Unshakable Belief System

So how do you build a belief system that can withstand the attacks?

Here are three practices that will anchor you:

1. Know Your "Why"
Your "why" is your purpose. When your "why" is clear, your "what" becomes easier. My "why" is breaking cycles and opening doors.

2. Feed Your Mind the Right Input
You become what you consume. Intentionally feed your mind truth, hope, and possibility through Scripture, leadership content, and stories of people who overcame adversity.

3. Anchor in Something Bigger Than Yourself
For me, it's God. For you, it might be purpose, legacy, or service. But it has to be bigger than you.

The H.O.P.E. Framework

Before we move to the B.A.T. in Practice section, I want to give you one more tool: the **H.O.P.E. Framework**.

H – **Humility:** Stay teachable and grounded.

O – **Optimism:** Believe that things can get better, even when circumstances shift.

P – **Purpose:** Know your "why" and let it anchor you.

E – **Empowerment:** Use your leadership to lift others. Your belief becomes stronger when you pour it into someone else.

When you lead with H.O.P.E., you become a dealer of hope for others.

B.A.T. in Practice: When Your Belief System Is Under Attack

Let me show you what this looks like in real life.

The Scenario:

You just got passed over for a promotion you thought you deserved. You've been working hard, putting in the hours, doing everything right. But they gave the role to someone else—someone less experienced, someone who hasn't proven themselves the way you have.

Your belief system is under attack.

The thoughts start flooding in:

"Maybe I'm not good enough."
"Maybe they were right about me all along."
"Maybe I should just accept that I'll never move up."
"Maybe I don't belong here."

This is the moment where B.A.T. becomes critical.

Here's how the three pillars show up when your belief is tested:

Belief: Anchor Back to Your Core

When your circumstances try to rewrite your identity, you have to anchor back to your values and your "why."

Ask yourself:

- *What do I know to be true about who I am—regardless of this setback?*
- *What are my core values? Have they changed because I didn't get this promotion?*
- *Who have I chosen to be as a person? Does that change based on one decision someone else made?*

The truth is:

You are capable. You are qualified. You are worthy.

This setback doesn't rewrite your identity. It's a moment, not a verdict.

Anchor statement:

"I am equipped for the level I'm pursuing. This setback doesn't define me. This is preparation, not rejection."

Action: Take Ownership of What You Can Control

Now that you've anchored your belief, it's time to act.

Don't wallow. Don't spiral. Don't make excuses. Take intentional action.

Here's what that looks like:

1. Request feedback.
Schedule a meeting with the decision-maker. Ask (humbly and professionally): *"What can I do to position myself better for the next opportunity? What gaps do you see that I need to address?"*

2. Identify your development areas.
Be honest with yourself. Where do you need to grow? What skills, experiences, or relationships would make you a stronger candidate next time?

3. Create a 90-day development plan.
Don't just talk about growth—build a plan. What will you learn? Who will you connect with? What will you accomplish in the next 90 days to position yourself for the next opportunity?

4. Keep delivering excellence in your current role.
Don't let disappointment make you check out. Continue to perform at a high level. Your response to this setback will be noticed.

Remember:

Action creates momentum. And momentum creates opportunity.

Thought: Reframe the Narrative

Finally, you have to manage your mindset.

The way you *think* about this setback will determine whether it destroys you or develops you.

Here's the reframe:

Instead of: *"This is rejection."*
Choose: *"This is redirection. Maybe this role wasn't the right fit. Maybe something better is coming."*

Instead of: *"I'll never get promoted."*
Choose: *"This is preparation. I'm being refined for the next level."*

Instead of: *"They don't believe in me."*
Choose: *"I'm responsible for my own development. I don't need their validation to grow."*

Ask yourself:
"What's the lesson here? What is this experience trying to teach me that I need to learn before I step into the next level?"

Putting It All Together: B.A.T. in Real Time

Without B.A.T.:

You spiral into self-doubt. You stop trying. You become bitter. You disengage from your work. You carry resentment. And eventually, you prove right the very doubts you were afraid were true.

With B.A.T.:

You anchor in your belief. You take intentional action. You reframe the setback as preparation. You show up with excellence. You grow from the experience.

And six months later, when the next opportunity comes—or when a better opportunity presents itself—you're ready. Not just because you're qualified, but because you're *refined*.

That's B.A.T. in practice.

It's not theory. It's not motivational speaking. It's the operating system that carries you through the hardest moments of your leadership journey.

Before you move to the next chapter, take a moment to reflect:

1. **What are your core values?** Can you name them? Are you living them?
2. **What's anchoring your belief system right now?** Is it strong enough to hold you when life gets hard?
3. **What voices are you listening to?** Are they building you up or tearing you down?

Action Challenges

1. **Write down your top 5 values.** Make them visible. Reference them when making decisions this week.
2. **Identify one negative voice you need to mute.** It could be a person, a thought pattern, or even social media. Take one action this week to limit its influence.
3. **Find one person who needs to hear a message of belief this week.** Speak life into them. Be their Aunt Bob.

Belief is the foundation. But belief without action is just wishful thinking.

In the next chapter, we're going to talk about how to turn belief into consistent, disciplined action.

CHAPTER 4

Do It: The Discipline of Action

In the last chapter, we talked about belief—the foundation of who you are.

But here's the hard truth: **Belief without action is just wishful thinking.**

You can have the strongest values in the world. You can have unshakable faith. You can believe you're capable of greatness.

But if you don't *act* on that belief—if you don't translate it into consistent, disciplined action—nothing changes.

This is where most people fail.

They believe they can do more. They want to do more. They even talk about doing more.

But when it comes time to actually *do* the work—to show up, to be consistent, to sacrifice—they quit.

Action is the bridge between belief and results.

And in this chapter, I'm going to show you how to build that bridge.

What "Act Positive" Really Means

When Aunt Bob said "act positive," she wasn't talking about doing random acts of kindness or putting on a happy face.

She was talking about **discipline, consistency, and integrity in action.**

Act positive is about what you *do*—not just once, but every single day.

It's about:

- Showing up when you don't feel like it
- Keeping your commitments even when it's hard
- Doing the work even when no one's watching
- Serving others even when there's no immediate benefit to you
- Following through when it would be easier to quit

Action is the proof of belief.

Anyone can say they believe in something. But your actions reveal what you truly believe.

The Three Pillars of Action

When I talk about action, I'm talking about three core elements:

1. **Discipline** – Doing what needs to be done, whether you feel like it or not
2. **Consistency** – Showing up every single day, even when progress feels slow
3. **Service** – Using your action to lift others, not just yourself

Let's break each one down.

Discipline is the ability to do what needs to be done, even when you don't feel like doing it.

It's waking up early to work on your goals when your bed is calling you back.

It's keeping your commitment to your team even when you're exhausted.

It's saying no to distractions so you can say yes to what matters.

Discipline is the difference between dreamers and doers.

Everyone has dreams. Everyone has goals. Everyone has potential.

But only disciplined people turn potential into results.

Discipline Is a Muscle

Here's what most people don't understand about discipline: **It's not something you're born with. It's something you build.**

Discipline is like a muscle. The more you use it, the stronger it gets.

When I was in college, I had to build discipline just to survive. I worked while going to school full-time. I had to study when I was exhausted. I had to manage money when there was barely any to manage.

I didn't start out disciplined. I became disciplined because I had to.

And the more I practiced discipline in small areas, the easier it became to apply it in bigger areas.

Here's how to build discipline:

1. Start small.

Don't try to overhaul your entire life overnight. Pick one area where you want to be more disciplined and focus there.

2. Create systems, not goals.

Goals are what you want to achieve. Systems are the daily actions that get you there. Focus on the system, not just the outcome.

3. Remove friction.

Make it easier to do the right thing. If you want to work out in the morning, lay out your clothes the night before. If you want to eat healthier, prep your meals in advance.

4. Track your progress.

What gets measured gets managed. Keep track of your discipline. Celebrate the days you show up.

5. Expect resistance.

Discipline isn't comfortable. Your brain will resist it. That's normal. Do it anyway.

The Discipline That Built My Career

Let me tell you about the hardest two years of my professional life—and how discipline was the only thing that got me through.

It was just after my fifth year in the industry. You know what they say about the "five-year itch"—that point where employees start questioning what's next, weighing their options, looking for the next opportunity.

I felt it too.

After days of meditation, reflection, and weighing pros and cons, I made a decision: **I was going to pursue my MBA.**

The timing was terrible.

I'd just taken on a new role as an Agricultural Lender. If you've never worked in ag lending, let me explain the difference:

Mortgage lending is black and white. The guidelines are clear. The rules are defined.

Ag lending is 100 shades of gray. We lived in the gray with our product offerings. Every deal was custom. Every situation was unique.

And I was a city boy learning a foreign language.

Oh, and did I mention this was 2009-2011? **The Great Recession.**

So I was:

- Learning a completely new job
- Handling distressed loans and restructures
- Pursuing an MBA
- Trying to maintain some semblance of work-life balance

My schedule was insane.

But I knew if I didn't create a system, I'd drown.

So here's what I built:

Weekly MBA Routine:

- **Monday (after work):** Review weekly assignments, game plan, begin research
- **Tuesday (after work):** Continue research, begin mid-week assignments, engage in course discussion boards
- **Wednesday (after work):** Study, complete mid-week work
- **Thursday (after work):** Start working on 10+ page papers

- **Friday (after work):** Reply to discussion posts, then rest
- **Saturday:** Work on papers for 8-10 hours
- **Sunday:** Final review and submission

Daily Routine:

- **5:00 a.m.:** Wake up—prayer, meditation, Bible reading
- **6:00-7:00 a.m.:** Workout
- **7:00-7:35 a.m.:** Commute (listening to audiobooks, podcasts)
- **8:00 a.m.-5:00 p.m.:** Work (fully present, no distractions)
- **Evenings:** Family time, then finish school work if needed

This was two years straight.

The work varied depending on the subject. Some weeks were lighter. Some weeks I was writing 15-page financial analysis papers while managing a portfolio of distressed ag loans.

It was brutal. But it worked.

Not because I was smarter than anyone else. Not because I had more time.

But because **I built a system and I refused to break it.**

Here's what I learned:

Discipline isn't about doing more. It's about doing what matters, consistently, even when you're exhausted.

It's about creating systems that don't rely on motivation—because motivation fades. Systems don't.

And here's the payoff:

I graduated with nearly a 4.0 GPA. I maintained my performance at work. My family didn't fall apart. I actually became *stronger*—not weaker—through the process.

That's the power of discipline.

It doesn't eliminate the struggle. But it carries you through it.

The Cost of Indiscipline

Let me be blunt: **Indiscipline costs you everything.**

It costs you opportunities because you're not prepared when they come.

It costs you credibility because people can't count on you.

It costs you momentum because you keep starting and stopping.

It costs you respect—both from others and from yourself.

I've seen talented people waste their potential because they lacked discipline.

And I've seen average people achieve extraordinary things because they were relentlessly disciplined.

Talent is overrated. Discipline is underrated.

The Front-End Investment Principle

Let me share one of my core life philosophies—something I've learned over 43 years that applies to every area of life:

You either pay on the front end or the back end. And it's far more costly to pay on the back end.

I've seen this play out in all aspects of life:

- Career development
- Relationships
- Health
- Financial planning
- Personal growth

Sometimes the front-end investment seems large. It appears costly. It feels like too much, too soon.

But that's almost always an illusion.

The front end saves time over time.
It allows relationship value to compound.
It allows monetary value to compound.
It allows life sufferings and trauma to heal faster when you invest in help early.

The easiest thing in the world is to make excuses. And with excuses, we can easily talk ourselves out of doing the hard things.

Yet it's the hard things we do that cause us to make the greatest impact.

The MBA: A Front-End Investment That Changed Everything

Remember that MBA story I just told you? The brutal two-year grind of working full-time, learning ag lending, and pursuing my degree?

There was more of me that didn't want to do it.

The timing wasn't right. I didn't want to accrue more debt. My wife and I were barely making ends meet on one income. The list of excuses went on and on.

But I made the front-end investment anyway.

And that investment opened up opportunities I couldn't have imagined.

Here's what happened:

Immediately after completing my MBA, I was offered the opportunity to participate in a distinguished four-year leadership development program.

That program:

- Increased my relationship capital exponentially
- Expanded my leadership skills and credibility
- Positioned me as a trusted leader with our internal leadership team
- Connected me with executives and peers I never would have accessed otherwise
- Gave me the chance to work on several meaningful projects that played a key role in our organization's success

All because I decided to make that front-end investment.

In hindsight, if I'd waited 10 years, I would have lost precious time. I wouldn't have accomplished nearly as much in that window.

The front-end investment wasn't just about the degree. It was about positioning myself for the next level—before I felt fully ready.

The Leadership Program: When Front-End Investment Saved the Day

Let me give you another example of how front-end investment pays off in ways you can't predict.

That four-year leadership development program I mentioned? Here's how it was structured:

Years 1-2: Leading Managers
We learned the fundamentals of leading people who lead others.

Years 3-4: Leading Leaders
We stepped into strategic leadership—learning to lead at a higher level, influence across the organization, and execute complex initiatives.

At the start of year three—the "leading leaders" phase—our team was assigned the project:

Build a loan origination program that aligns people, process, and technology across multiple departments.

We had two years to bring it together, execute, and deliver.

Oh, and by the way—**we still had our day jobs.**

We were each maintaining our current responsibilities, taking care of customers, building our own business. This project was in addition to everything else on our plates.

Time was not our friend.

And the pressure? Let's just say we were a group of four overachievers who didn't do anything halfway. So the standards were high, the stakes were real, and the clock was ticking. role? I was responsible for the processes.

I was responsible for creating the loan flow through the tech — mapping out how each role connected, where people started and stopped, when and where to communicate, who to involve and when, and determining what was needed at each stage.

It was like building a roadmap for dozens of people across multiple departments who'd never worked together this way before.

And let me tell you: the entire project was brutal.

(And I mean that in the most loving, character-building way possible.)

Late nights. Long discussions—some of which felt like diplomatic negotiations. Stress. Endless meetings. Collaborations where we'd debate the definition of a single word for 45 minutes. Training sessions. Building technology. Writing manuals. Creating flowcharts that looked like subway maps.

Every detail mattered. If loan officers didn't know when to hand off to processors, deals stalled. If processors didn't know when to involve closers, deadlines were missed. If operations didn't know their touchpoints, the whole system broke down.

Our team of four worked through every scenario, every edge case, every "what if" question you could imagine—and a few you couldn't.

To be honest, there were moments when I didn't know how we were going to pull it off.

Two years sounds like a lot of time—until you're juggling a full-time leadership role, a customer portfolio, and a project that requires rebuilding how an entire organization operates.

But we kept showing up. We kept pushing. We kept believing it was possible.

And at the end of 2019, we delivered.

(Cue collective sigh of relief.)

And then, three months later, COVID-19 hit.

Suddenly, most of our staff was working from home. But we still needed to take care of our customers—farmers and agricultural producers who play a critical role in providing food and fiber to the world.

And you know what saved us?

That tech platform we'd just built. Those process flows we'd mapped out.

All those late nights. All those "diplomatic negotiations." All that front-end investment in technology, training, and systems—it was delivered just in time.

Our staff was able to use the platform while working from home. Loan officers, processors, closers, operations teams—everyone could work cross-functionally and communicate seamlessly, even though they were scattered across the state.

They knew exactly where they fit in the process. They knew who to communicate with. They knew what was needed at each stage.

Without that tech—and without those process flows—there's no way we would have been able to keep business moving forward.

It wasn't perfect. But it forced us to work together as a team and to learn by doing.

And it happened because **we** made the front-end investment before we knew we'd need it.

The Lesson: Do Your Part, Make the Front-End Investment

Here's what I want you to take away from this:

The front-end investment always feels harder than waiting.

It feels costly. It feels inconvenient. It feels like bad timing.

But the back-end cost—the cost of waiting, of procrastinating, of avoiding the hard thing—is always higher.

When you invest on the front end:

- You position yourself for opportunities you can't yet see
- You build skills and relationships that compound over time
- You create systems that carry you through crises you can't predict
- You prove to yourself—and others—that you're someone who does hard things

It takes everyone to make the magic happen. But you have to do your part.

Make that front-end investment every day.

And do it with a B.A.T. Positive attitude.

Because the hard things you do today are the breakthroughs you'll celebrate tomorrow.

Pillar 2: Consistency - Showing Up Every Single Day

Discipline gets you started. Consistency keeps you going.

Consistency is doing the right thing over and over again, even when you don't see immediate results.

This is where most people quit.

They start strong. They're motivated. They're excited.

But when the results don't come as quickly as they hoped, they lose momentum. They start skipping days. They make excuses. And eventually, they quit.

Here's what I've learned: Success isn't built in the big moments. It's built in the small, unsexy, repetitive actions that nobody sees.

It's the daily discipline of:

- Showing up on time
- Doing your job well
- Keeping your commitments
- Following through
- Learning and growing
- Serving others

Those small actions compound over time.

And eventually, they create extraordinary results.

The Compound Effect

There's a principle I live by called **the compound effect.**

It's the idea that small, consistent actions—repeated over time—create exponential results.

Think of it like this:

If you get 1% better every day for a year, you'll be 37 times better by the end of the year.

If you get 1% worse every day for a year, you'll decline to nearly zero.

The difference between success and failure isn't one big decision. It's the accumulation of small decisions made consistently over time.

This is true in every area of life:

In your career: Showing up with excellence every day builds a reputation that opens doors.

In your health: Working out consistently, even when you don't feel like it, transforms your body over time.

In your relationships: Small acts of love and service, repeated daily, build deep, lasting bonds.

In your leadership: Consistent integrity, consistent communication, consistent follow-through—that's what builds trust.

You don't need to be perfect. You just need to be consistent.

The Year I Showed Up and Nothing Happened

Let me tell you about my first year as a mortgage lender—when I was convinced I wasn't cut out for the job.

It was heavy sales. Sink or swim. And I was drowning.

The mortgage industry was oversaturated. Everyone was offering the same products. But we had a niche—rural property financing. That was our edge.

So I set out to build relationships with realtors. I visited offices all over Winston-Salem.

I'll never forget the first company I walked into. As I was coming through the front door, several realtors were walking out the back.

I stood there in the lobby, waiting for someone—anyone—to appear.

Nobody came.

So I left my business card on the counter and headed to the next one.

That became the pattern. Knocking on doors. Leaving cards. Hearing crickets.

The reality was, most realtors had their established relationships. And I was the new kid on the block. Green. Unproven.

Months went by. No deals.

I was frustrated. Discouraged. I started thinking maybe I wasn't cut out for this.

Then one day, my boss stopped by the office while passing through on a business trip.

He took me to lunch. And he said something I'll never forget:

"Lance, hang in there. I see leadership qualities in you. I see a bright future. You're doing all the right things. You don't have anything to worry about—just keep doing what you're doing."

That conversation changed everything.

It didn't change my circumstances. I still didn't have deals coming in.

But it changed my belief. It gave me the fuel to keep showing up.

And then, something shifted.

Deals started coming. Slowly at first. Then more consistently.

I started supporting clients. Building my book of business. Earning trust.

By the end of that year, I was recognized as the **Winston-Salem Mortgage Lender Rookie of the Year.**

Here's what I learned:

1. You have to pay your dues.
Success doesn't just show up. You have to do the work—even when nobody's watching, even when results aren't immediate.

2. Every action is moving you closer.
Even when it doesn't feel like it. Even when you're walking into empty lobbies and leaving business cards nobody reads.

3. Others are watching how you handle adversity.
My boss saw something in me during those months of struggle. He saw consistency. He saw resilience. And that's what he invested in.

Consistency doesn't guarantee instant results. But it always produces eventual results.

The difference between success and failure is often just showing up longer than everyone else is willing to.

When Consistency Feels Impossible

Let's be real: There will be days when showing up feels impossible.

Days when you're exhausted.

Days when you're discouraged.

Days when you don't see progress and you wonder if it's even worth it.

I've had those days. Many of them.

Here's what I do when consistency feels hard:

1. I remember my "why."
Why did I start this? What's the bigger purpose? Who's counting on me?

2. I focus on just today.
I don't worry about tomorrow or next week. I just ask: *Can I show up today?*

3. I lower the bar.
If I can't do 100%, I do 50%. If I can't do 50%, I do 10%. But I show up.

4. I lean on my systems.
I don't rely on motivation. I rely on the habits and routines I've built.

5. I remind myself: This is where everyone else quits.
The days when it's hardest to show up are the days that separate the good from the great.

Consistency isn't about being perfect. It's about refusing to quit.

Pillar 3: Service - Using Your Action to Lift Others

The third pillar of action is service.

True leadership is service.

It's using your gifts, your resources, your position, and your influence to lift others.

Aunt Bob modeled this for me. She didn't have much, but she gave everything she had to raise five boys who weren't her responsibility.

She took us to the nursing home every Christmas season to serve people who had been forgotten.

She taught us that **service isn't about what you have. It's about what you give.**

Service Builds Character

Here's something I learned early: **The fastest way to grow as a leader is to serve others.**

When you serve, you develop:

Empathy – You learn to see the world through someone else's eyes.

Humility – You realize it's not about you. It's about the mission and the people you're serving.

Patience – You learn that growth takes time, both for you and for the people you're investing in.

Gratitude – You realize how much you've been given and how much you have to offer.

Service shifts your focus from "What can I get?" to "What can I give?"

And that shift changes everything.

A Personal Example of Service

Early in my management career, I had a young lender on my team who was struggling. She was talented, but she lacked confidence. She second-guessed every decision. She was afraid to take risks.

I could have written her off. I could have focused my energy on the top performers who didn't need as much attention.

But I chose to invest in her.

I met with her weekly. I coached her through difficult situations. I gave her stretch assignments that forced her to grow. I celebrated her small wins publicly.

It took time. It took energy. And there were moments when I wondered if it was worth it.

But years later, she's now one of the top producers in her region. She's confident, capable, and developing others the way I developed her.

That's the power of service.

When you invest in people—when you serve them without expecting anything in return—you create a ripple effect that extends far beyond what you can see.

Service When It Cost Me

Let me tell you about a time when service required real sacrifice.

I had a team member—let's call him Marcus—who was struggling both personally and professionally. His performance was declining. He was missing deadlines. He wasn't responding to coaching.

Most leaders would have started the termination process. And honestly, I considered it.

But I felt like there was something deeper going on.

So I sat down with him and asked: *"Marcus, what's really happening? This isn't like you."*

He broke down. His family was going through a crisis. He was trying to be there for them while maintaining his workload. He was drowning.

I had a choice: I could hold him to the standard and start the performance improvement process. Or I could serve him in his season of crisis.

I chose to serve.

I adjusted his workload temporarily. I brought in support from other team members. I checked in with him weekly—not about work, but about life.

It cost me.

I had to redistribute work to an already-busy team. I had to explain to my boss why Marcus's numbers were down. I had to extend grace when policy said I shouldn't.

But here's what happened: Marcus's family situation improved. Marcus returned to full strength. And he became one of the most loyal, high-performing members of my team.

Years later, he told me: *"You didn't just manage me. You saw me. And that changed everything."*

That's service. It's costly. But it's worth it.

How to Serve as a Leader

So how do you lead through service?

Here are five practical ways:

1. Serve your team before yourself.
Ask: *What do my team members need to succeed? How can I remove obstacles for them?*

2. Invest in people who can't immediately benefit you.
Mentor someone who's just starting out. Open a door for someone who doesn't have access. Give your time to someone who can't pay you back.

3. Do the work nobody else wants to do.
Don't ask your team to do something you're not willing to do yourself. Lead by example.

4. Celebrate others' wins.
Make sure your team gets the credit when things go well. Share the spotlight.

5. Stay humble.
Remember where you came from. Remember who invested in you. And pay it forward.

Service isn't weakness. It's strength.

The Enemies of Action

Just like belief has enemies, so does action.

Here are the three biggest enemies of action:

Enemy 1: Procrastination

Procrastination is the killer of dreams.

It's the voice that says, "I'll start tomorrow." "I'll do it when I have more time." "I'll wait until conditions are perfect."

But perfect conditions never come.

And tomorrow becomes next week. Next week becomes next month. Next month becomes never.

Here's the truth: You don't need perfect conditions to start. You just need to start.

Action creates clarity. Momentum creates motivation.

Stop waiting for the perfect moment. The moment is now.

Enemy 2: Fear of Failure

The second enemy of action is fear.

Fear of failing. Fear of looking foolish. Fear of being judged.

But here's what I've learned: Failure is not the opposite of success. It's part of the process.

Every successful person you admire has failed. Multiple times.

The difference is, they didn't let failure stop them. They learned from it and kept moving.

Failure is feedback. Use it.

Enemy 3: Excuses

The third enemy of action is excuses.

"I don't have time."
"I don't have the resources."
"I don't have the right connections."
"I'm too old." "I'm too young."
"I don't have the experience."

Excuses are easy. Action is hard.

But here's the reality: **Excuses don't change your situation. Action does.**

You can make excuses, or you can make progress. But you can't do both.

Building a Life of Action

So how do you build a life defined by disciplined, consistent, service-oriented action?

Here are three practices that will help:

1. Start Before You're Ready
You'll never feel 100% ready. Start anyway. Imperfect action beats perfect inaction every time.

2. Build Systems, Not Just Goals
Goals tell you where you want to go. Systems tell you how to get there.

Focus on building daily habits and routines that move you toward your goals.

3. Find an Accountability Partner

You can't do this alone. Find someone who will check in on you, challenge you, and celebrate with you.

B.A.T. in Practice: When You Don't Feel Like Showing Up

Let me show you what B.A.T. looks like when action is the hardest thing to do.

The Scenario:

You're exhausted. You've been grinding for months—maybe years. You're pouring everything into your work, your team, your goals. But you're not seeing the results you expected.

Your team isn't responding the way you hoped. Your boss isn't recognizing your effort. The project you've been leading is stalling. You're starting to question whether any of it matters.

And this morning, you woke up and thought: *I don't want to do this today.*

This is the moment where action becomes the differentiator.

Because here's the truth: Everyone feels this way sometimes. The difference between average and great isn't talent—it's what you do on the days you don't feel like showing up.

Here's how B.A.T. carries you through:

Belief: Remember Your "Why"

When you don't feel like acting, reconnect with your belief system.

Ask yourself:

- *Why did I start this in the first place?*
- *What's the mission I'm serving?*
- *Who's depending on me to keep going?*

The truth is:
Your feelings are real. Your exhaustion is valid. But your purpose is bigger than your feelings.

You didn't start this journey for easy days. You started it because it mattered. And it still matters—even on the days when you don't *feel* like it matters.

Anchor statement:
"I'm tired, but I'm not done. My 'why' is bigger than my weariness. I will show up today—not because it's easy, but because it's necessary."

Action: Do the Next Right Thing

You don't have to do everything today. You don't have to solve every problem. You don't have to be perfect.

You just have to do the *next right thing.*

Here's what that looks like:

1. Identify one small action you can take today.
What's the one thing that, if you did it, would move the needle forward? Do that. Just that.

2. Break the big goal into micro-steps.

Overwhelm kills action. Instead of thinking, "I have to turn this whole project around," think, "I'm going to send one email. I'm going to have one conversation. I'm going to complete one task."

3. Show up for your team—even if you don't show up for yourself.

Sometimes the only reason you show up is because other people are counting on you. And that's okay. Leadership is service. Serve today, even if you don't feel inspired.

4. Celebrate the small win.

When you complete that one task, acknowledge it. Don't dismiss it. You showed up. You acted. That's a win.

Remember:

Momentum builds from small actions. You don't need to run a marathon today. You just need to take one step.

Thought: Reframe Exhaustion as Investment

Now, let's manage your mindset.

When you're exhausted, your mind will try to convince you that the effort isn't worth it. That you're wasting your time. That nothing is changing.

Here's the reframe:

Instead of: *"I'm tired of this. It's not working."*
Choose: *"I'm investing in something that takes time. Growth isn't linear."*

Instead of: *"Nobody appreciates what I'm doing."*
Choose: *"I'm not doing this for applause. I'm doing this because it aligns with my values."*

Instead of: *"I don't have the energy for this."*
Choose: *"I'm building stamina. Every day I show up, I'm getting stronger."*

Ask yourself:
"What will I regret more—showing up tired today, or quitting and looking back with regret tomorrow?"

Putting It All Together: B.A.T. in Real Time

Without B.A.T.:
You give in to the exhaustion. You skip the workout. You avoid the hard conversation. You let the day slip by without progress. And the guilt compounds the exhaustion. Tomorrow becomes even harder.

With B.A.T.:
You reconnect with your "why." You take one small action. You reframe exhaustion as investment. You show up—not perfectly, but consistently.

And weeks later, you look back and realize: those hard days were the ones that mattered most. Those were the days that built your character, your resilience, your discipline.

That's B.A.T. in practice.

It's showing up on the days you don't feel like it. It's choosing action over comfort. It's understanding that consistency beats intensity every single time.

Before you move to the next chapter, take a moment to reflect:

1. **Where do you need more discipline in your life?** What's one area where you know you're capable of more, but you're not showing up consistently?
2. **What's your biggest obstacle to action?** Is it procrastination? Fear? Excuses? What's one thing you can do this week to overcome it?
3. **Who are you serving?** How are you using your actions to lift others, not just yourself?

Action Challenges

1. **Identify one area where you need to build discipline.** Commit to showing up in that area every day for the next 7 days. Track your progress.
2. **Create a system for one of your goals.** Instead of just setting a goal, build a daily routine that supports it.
3. **Serve someone this week who can't immediately benefit you.** Mentor, coach, encourage, or support someone who's earlier in their journey than you.

Belief anchors you. Action moves you forward. But if your thoughts are working against you, you'll sabotage everything you're building.

In the next chapter, we're going to talk about how to master your mindset—so your thoughts work for you, not against you.

CHAPTER 5

Think It: The Mastery of Mindset

We've covered belief and action. Now it's time to talk about the third pillar: **thought.**

Belief is who you are.
Action is what you do.
Thought is how you think—and how you think determines everything.

You can have strong values. You can take consistent action. But if your internal dialogue is negative, toxic, or defeatist, you'll sabotage everything you're building.

Your mindset is either your greatest asset or your greatest liability.

And here's the beautiful—and terrifying—truth: **You get to choose.**

You can't always control what happens to you. But you can always control how you think about what happens to you.

That's the power of mindset.

What "Think Positive" Really Means

When Aunt Bob said "think positive," she wasn't asking me to ignore reality or pretend everything was fine.

She was teaching me about **perspective, resilience, and mental discipline.**

Think positive is about **how you frame adversity, manage your internal dialogue, and choose what you focus on.**

It's about:

- Reframing setbacks as opportunities
- Managing negative self-talk
- Focusing on what you can control instead of what you can't
- Choosing gratitude over bitterness
- Seeing possibility when others see obstacles

Your thoughts create your reality.

Not in some magical, manifestation way. But in a very real, practical way.

What you think about shapes what you believe. What you believe shapes what you do. What you do shapes your outcomes.

If you want to change your life, start by changing your thoughts.

The Power of Perspective

One of the most powerful lessons I've learned is this: **Two people can experience the exact same situation and come away with completely different stories.**

One person sees failure. The other sees feedback.

One person sees rejection. The other sees redirection.

One person sees a setback. The other sees preparation for the next level.

The difference isn't the situation. It's the perspective.

Let me give you an example from my own life.

The Job I Didn't Get

Early in my career, I applied for a position I desperately wanted. I was qualified. I'd put in the work. I'd built relationships. I was confident I'd get it.

But I didn't.

They gave it to someone else.

In that moment, I had a choice.

I could think: *"They don't believe in me. I'm not good enough. This organization doesn't value me."*

Or I could think: *"This wasn't the right opportunity. Something better is coming. What's the lesson here?"*

I chose the second perspective.

And here's what happened: Six months later, a better opportunity opened up. One that was a better fit for my skills, my values, and my long-term goals.

If I had gotten that first job, I wouldn't have been positioned for the second one.

Looking back, I can see that the rejection was redirection.

But I only see that now because I chose to think about it differently in the moment.

Your perspective determines your trajectory.

Reframing in Real Time: The Presentation I'll Never Forget

Let me tell you about the time I got absolutely dismantled by a senior executive—and how reframing saved me.

I was presenting a new lending program to leadership. I'd spent months developing it. I believed it could be transformational.

My strategy? Meet with each executive leader separately. Build consensus one-on-one before taking it to the full team.

Smart, right?

Well, the second leader I met with had a different idea.

I walked in thinking I'd gloss over the details, keep it high-level, get a quick nod of approval.

That leader had other plans.

They picked my presentation apart. Line by line. Assumption by assumption.

"Where's the data to support this?"
"Have you considered the impact on X?"
"What about Y? Did you think about Z?"

I was sweating. Stumbling. Backpedaling.

And then, right when I thought it couldn't get worse, the leader looked at me and said:

"I bet you didn't expect this."

(Cue nervous laughter.)

No. No, I did not.

I walked out of that office feeling like I'd just been through a professional boxing match. And I'd lost. Badly.

My first thought was: *"I just embarrassed myself. My credibility is shot."*

But then I caught myself.

I could either spiral into shame and defeat, or I could reframe this as a gift.

Old frame: *"I failed. That leader doesn't respect me."*
New frame: *"That leader just gave me a masterclass in executive-level thinking. For free."*

Old frame: *"My proposal was destroyed."*
New frame: *"My proposal has gaps I didn't see. Now I know exactly what to fix."*

Old frame: *"I'm not ready for this level of leadership."*
New frame: *"This is what growth looks like. I just got stronger."*

Within 30 minutes of leaving that office, I'd reframed the entire experience.

And here's what I did next:

I went back to my office. I rewrote the proposal. I anticipated every question. I considered every outcome from a 360-degree perspective. I connected dots I hadn't seen before. I over-prepared like my career depended on it.

Because it did.

Three months later, I came back with a revised proposal.

And it was approved.

Here's what that experience taught me:

1. Never underestimate your audience.
I walked in thinking I could wing it. That leader reminded me that excellence requires preparation.

2. Tough feedback is a gift—if you reframe it.
That leader could have just said "no" and moved on. Instead, they invested time in showing me what I was missing. That's leadership.

3. Reframing happens in real time.
You don't have to wait weeks or months to shift your perspective. You can do it in the moment. And that's when it's most powerful.

If I'd let my initial thoughts win—if I'd spiraled into shame—I would have quit.

But reframing kept me in the game. And eventually, it got me the win.

When I talk about mindset, I'm talking about three core elements:

1. **Self-Talk** – The internal dialogue you have with yourself
2. **Focus** – What you choose to pay attention to
3. **Gratitude** – The practice of acknowledging what's working, not just what's broken

Let's break each one down.

Element 1: Self-Talk - The Conversation That Shapes Your Life

Self-talk is the voice in your head. The running commentary you have about yourself, your circumstances, and your future.

And for most people, that voice is brutal.

It tells you you're not good enough. That you're falling behind. That you don't have what it takes. That you'll never measure up.

If you spoke to your friends the way you speak to yourself, you'd have no friends.

But here's the truth: **Your self-talk is trainable.**

You can change the narrative. You can replace destructive thoughts with empowering ones.

It takes discipline. But it's possible.

The Two Types of Self-Talk

There are two types of self-talk:

1. Fixed Mindset Self-Talk

This is the voice that says:

- "I'm not good at this."
- "I always fail."
- "I'm just not that kind of person."
- "This is too hard for me."

Fixed mindset self-talk assumes you can't change. That you are who you are, and that's that.

2. Growth Mindset Self-Talk

This is the voice that says:

- "I'm not good at this *yet*."
- "I failed, but I learned something."
- "I'm becoming that kind of person."
- "This is hard, but I can figure it out."

Growth mindset self-talk assumes you can learn, grow, and improve.

The difference between these two mindsets determines everything.

How to Change Your Self-Talk

So how do you shift from fixed mindset to growth mindset?

Here's a simple framework:

Step 1: Notice the thought.
The first step is awareness. You can't change what you don't notice. Pay attention to your internal dialogue.

Step 2: Challenge the thought.
Ask yourself: *Is this thought true? Is it helpful? Is it empowering?*

Step 3: Replace the thought.
If the thought isn't true, helpful, or empowering, replace it with one that is.

Example:

Negative thought: *"I'm terrible at public speaking."*

Challenge: *Is that true? Or am I just inexperienced? Can I get better with practice?*

Replacement: *"I'm not great at public speaking yet, but I'm improving every time I do it."*

That one shift—from "I'm terrible" to "I'm improving"—changes everything.

The Night I Almost Quit

Let me tell you about a night when my thoughts almost convinced me to walk away from everything.

It was during my time as Regional Lending Manager. I'd been in the role for about six months, and I was struggling.

I was dealing with underperforming team members. I was navigating organizational politics. I was trying to prove I deserved the position while carrying the weight of being "the first."

And one night, after a particularly brutal day, I sat in my car in the parking lot and thought: *Maybe they were right. Maybe I'm not cut out for this.*

The negative self-talk was relentless:

"You're in over your head."
"Your team doesn't respect you."
"You only got this job because of diversity quotas."
"You're going to fail, and everyone will say they knew it all along."

I called my wife. I told her I was thinking about stepping down.

And you know what she said?

"Lance, those thoughts aren't truth. They're fear. And if you let fear make this decision, you'll regret it for the rest of your life."

She was right.

So I did what I'm teaching you to do: I separated the thought from the truth.

The thought said: *"You're failing."*
The truth was: *"You're learning. This is hard because you've never done it before. Give yourself grace."*

The thought said: *"Your team doesn't respect you."*
The truth was: *"Some team members are resistant to change. That's normal. Keep showing up with integrity."*

The thought said: *"You don't belong here."*
The truth was: *"You earned this. And you're exactly where you need to be."*

That night, I made a decision: **I would not let my thoughts write my story.**

I stayed. I fought through. I led with everything I had.

And six months later, the team was thriving. The results were there. And I realized: the only thing that almost stopped me was my own mind.

That's why mastering your mindset isn't optional. It's survival.

Element 2: Focus - What You Pay Attention To

The second element of mindset is focus.

What you focus on expands.

If you focus on what's broken, you'll see brokenness everywhere.

If you focus on what's possible, you'll see opportunity everywhere.

Your focus determines your reality.

The Reticular Activating System (RAS)

There's a part of your brain called the **Reticular Activating System (RAS)**. It's a filter that determines what information gets through to your conscious awareness.

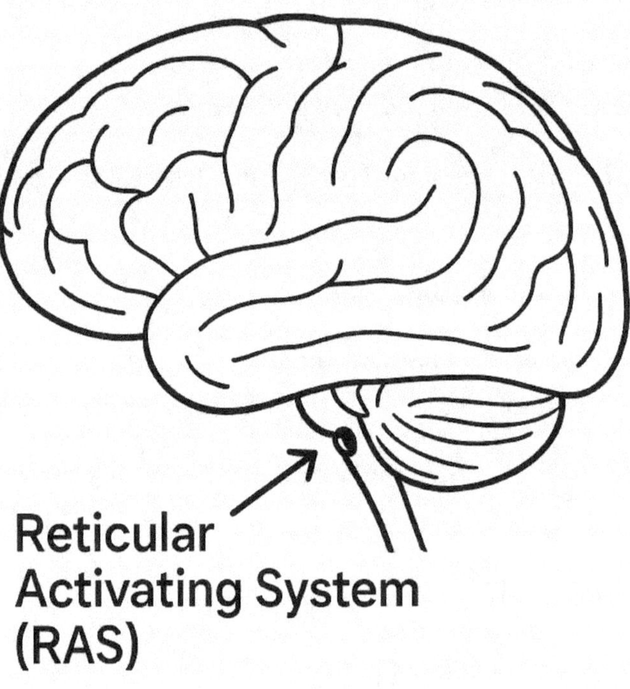

The Reticular Activating System (RAS) filters information, allowing you to focus on what you've programmed your brain to notice.

Here's how it works:

Have you ever bought a new car, and then suddenly you start seeing that same car everywhere?

The car was always there. But now that you own it, your brain is tuned to notice it.

That's your RAS at work.

And here's the key: **Your RAS is programmable.**

Whatever you tell your brain to focus on, it will find evidence for.

If you tell your brain, *"Life is hard. Nothing works out for me,"* your RAS will filter information to confirm that belief. You'll notice every setback, every disappointment, every obstacle.

But if you tell your brain, *"I'm capable. Opportunities are everywhere. I can figure this out,"* your RAS will filter information to confirm *that* belief. You'll notice possibilities, resources, and solutions.

You don't change what's out there. You change what you focus on.

Where to Focus Your Attention

So where should you focus?

Here are three principles:

1. Focus on what you can control.
You can't control the economy, your boss's mood, or what other people think of you. But you can control your effort, your attitude, and your response.

2. Focus on progress, not perfection.
Perfectionism is paralyzing. Progress is empowering. Celebrate the small wins. Acknowledge the growth.

3. Focus on solutions, not problems.
Problems are inevitable. But if you spend all your time focused on the problem, you'll never find the solution. Shift your focus to: *What can I do about this?*

What you focus on, you move toward.

Element 3: Gratitude - The Antidote to Bitterness

The third element of mindset is gratitude.

Gratitude is not just a nice feeling. It's a strategic practice.

When you practice gratitude, you train your brain to focus on what's working instead of what's broken.

And when you focus on what's working, you create momentum. You build resilience. You shift from scarcity to abundance.

Gratitude doesn't ignore the hard stuff. It just refuses to let the hard stuff be the only story.

The Science of Gratitude

There's real science behind gratitude.

Research shows that people who regularly practice gratitude:

- Have lower levels of stress and depression
- Sleep better
- Have stronger immune systems
- Build more resilient relationships
- Experience greater life satisfaction

Gratitude literally rewires your brain.

When you practice gratitude consistently, you strengthen the neural pathways associated with positive emotions. Over time, your brain becomes better at noticing the good instead of defaulting to the negative.

Gratitude is a discipline. And like any discipline, it gets easier with practice.

My Personal Gratitude Practice

Here's exactly how I practice gratitude:

Morning Routine (5 minutes):

- Before I check my phone, I write down three things I'm grateful for
- I make them specific: "I'm grateful for my wife's support yesterday when I was stressed" (not just "my wife")
- I feel it—I don't just write it. I let the gratitude sit in my chest for 30 seconds

During Tough Moments:

- When something frustrating happens, I ask: *"What's one thing I can be grateful for right now?"*
- Example: Stuck in traffic → "I'm grateful I have a car and a job to drive to"
- Example: Difficult team member → "I'm grateful this is teaching me patience"

Weekly Review (Sunday nights):

- I review the week and identify three wins (even small ones)
- I text or call someone who contributed to those wins and thank them

That's it. Nothing complicated. Just consistent.

And over time, it's rewired my brain to see opportunity instead of obstacles.

The Enemies of Mindset

Just like belief and action have enemies, so does mindset.

Here are the three biggest enemies of a positive mindset:

Enemy 1: Negative Self-Talk

We've already talked about this, but it's worth repeating: **Negative self-talk is toxic.**

If left unchecked, it will destroy your confidence, erode your belief, and sabotage your action.

You have to manage your internal dialogue intentionally.

Enemy 2: Comparison

Comparison is the thief of joy—and the killer of mindset.

When you compare your beginning to someone else's middle, you'll always feel inadequate.

When you measure your Chapter 2 against someone else's Chapter 10, you'll always feel behind.

Stop comparing. Start competing with yourself.

Ask: *Am I better today than I was yesterday? Am I growing? Am I moving forward?*

That's the only comparison that matters.

Enemy 3: Dwelling on the Past

The third enemy of mindset is dwelling on past failures, mistakes, or regrets.

Your past is data, not destiny. It's feedback, not a life sentence.

You can't change what happened. But you can change what you do next.

Stop replaying yesterday. Start planning tomorrow.

Building a Resilient Mindset

So how do you build a mindset that's resilient, empowering, and focused on possibility?

Here are three practices:

1. Feed Your Mind the Right Input

You become what you consume. Intentionally feed your mind truth, hope, and possibility through books, podcasts, conversations with people who believe in you, and content that aligns with your values.

2. Reframe Adversity

Every challenge is an opportunity to practice reframing. When something doesn't go your way, ask: *What's the lesson here? What's the opportunity? How is this preparing me for what's next?*

3. Practice Gratitude Daily

Make gratitude a non-negotiable part of your routine. Every morning or evening, write down three things you're grateful for. Gratitude shifts your focus from scarcity to abundance.

B.A.T. in Practice: When Negative Thoughts Are Winning

Let me show you what B.A.T. looks like when your mind is working against you.

The Scenario:

You just made a mistake. A big one.

You said the wrong thing in a meeting. You missed a critical deadline. You made a decision that backfired. And now you're replaying it over and over in your head.

"I can't believe I did that."
"Everyone probably thinks I'm incompetent."
"I'm never going to recover from this."
"Maybe I'm not cut out for this role."

The negative self-talk is loud. It's relentless. And it's starting to convince you that maybe it's true.

This is the moment where mastering your mindset becomes critical.

Because here's the reality: You will make mistakes. You will have bad days. You will say the wrong thing, make the wrong call, and wish you could go back and do it differently.

But the way you think about those moments determines whether they break you or build you.

Here's how B.A.T. shows up when your thoughts are working against you:

Belief: Separate the Event from Your Identity

When you make a mistake, your mind will try to turn it into an identity statement.

The mistake says: *"You messed up."*
Your mind says: *"You're a mess-up."*

But here's the truth:
You are not your mistake. You made a mistake. There's a difference.

Ask yourself:

- *Does this one mistake erase all the good work I've done?*
- *Does this moment define my entire character and capability?*
- *If a friend made this same mistake, would I write them off—or would I encourage them to learn and grow?*

The truth is:

You are capable. You are learning. You are human.

This mistake doesn't rewrite your identity. It's a moment of growth, not a final verdict.

Anchor statement:

"I made a mistake, but I am not a mistake. I am learning. I am growing. This moment does not define me."

Action: Own It, Learn From It, Move Forward

Now that you've anchored your belief, it's time to take action.

Don't spiral. Don't hide. Don't pretend it didn't happen. Own it, extract the lesson, and move forward.

Here's what that looks like:

1. Acknowledge the mistake publicly (if necessary).

If your mistake affected others, own it. Say: *"I made a mistake. Here's what happened, here's what I'm learning, and here's how I'm going to make it right."*

Owning your mistakes builds trust. Hiding them destroys it.

2. Extract the lesson.

Don't waste the mistake. Ask yourself:

- *What did this teach me?*
- *What would I do differently next time?*
- *What system or process can I put in place to prevent this from happening again?*

3. Make it right (if possible).

If there's something you can do to correct the mistake, do it. Apologize if needed. Fix what can be fixed. Take responsibility.

4. Move forward.

Don't camp out in guilt. You've acknowledged it. You've learned from it. Now move forward.

Remember:

Mistakes are not the end. They're data. They're feedback. They're preparation for the next opportunity.

Thought: Reframe the Mistake as Growth

Finally, you have to manage your internal dialogue.

The way you *think* about this mistake will determine whether it paralyzes you or propels you forward.

Here's the reframe:

Instead of: *"I'm so stupid. I can't believe I did that."*
Choose: *"I'm learning. This is part of the process. Every expert was once a beginner who made mistakes."*

Instead of: *"Everyone thinks I'm incompetent now."*
Choose: *"People respect leaders who own their mistakes and grow from them. This is an opportunity to build credibility, not lose it."*

Instead of: *"I'll never recover from this."*
Choose: *"This mistake doesn't define my career. How I respond to it will."*

Ask yourself:
"What's the most empowering way I can think about this situation? What story do I want to tell myself about this moment?"

Putting It All Together: B.A.T. in Real Time

Without B.A.T.:
You spiral into negative self-talk. You replay the mistake endlessly. You avoid the people involved. You let shame and guilt consume you. You start to believe the lie that you're not capable. And the mistake becomes a self-fulfilling prophecy.

With B.A.T.:
You separate the mistake from your identity. You own it, learn from it, and move forward. You reframe it as growth. You show up the next day with humility and resilience.

And six months later, you look back and realize: that mistake was a turning point. It taught you something critical. It made you a better leader.

That's B.A.T. in practice.

It's not avoiding mistakes—it's managing your mind when you make them. It's choosing empowering thoughts over destructive ones. It's understanding that your internal dialogue is the most powerful conversation you'll ever have.

Reflection Questions

Before you move to the next chapter, take a moment to reflect:

1. **What's your dominant self-talk?** Is it empowering or destructive? What's one negative thought pattern you need to change?
2. **What are you focusing on?** Are you focused on what you can control or what you can't? On problems or solutions?
3. **What are you grateful for?** Can you name three things right now?

Action Challenges

1. **Start a gratitude journal.** For the next 7 days, write down three things you're grateful for each day.
2. **Identify one negative thought pattern you need to reframe.** Write down the negative thought, challenge it, and replace it with an empowering one.
3. **Limit your consumption of negativity.** Choose one source of negativity (news, social media, toxic relationship) and reduce or eliminate it this week.

Belief anchors you. Action moves you forward. Thought sustains you.

Now it's time to see how all three pillars come together in real-world leadership.

PART 3: LEADERSHIP

CHAPTER 6

B.A.T. in Leadership: From Entry-Level to Senior Leadership

If you've made it this far, you understand the framework.

Belief sets your foundation. It's who you are at your core—your values, your character, your anchor.

Action is the centerpiece. It's what you do every single day—the discipline, the consistency, the service, the sacrifice.

Thought is what sustains you. It's how you manage your mind, reframe adversity, and choose to see opportunity instead of obstacles.

But here's the question: **How do you apply B.A.T. Positive in real-world leadership?**

How do you use this framework when you're managing difficult employees? When you're navigating organizational politics? When you're trying to build a positive team culture in a negative environment?

That's what this chapter is about.

This is where I take you inside my nearly 20-year journey in agricultural finance—from entry-level loan officer to senior leadership. This is where I show you how B.A.T. Positive carried me through every challenge, every promotion, every setback, and every breakthrough.

And more importantly, this is where I show you how to apply it in your leadership journey—no matter where you are or where you're trying to go.

Let's dive in.

The Journey: From Loan Officer to Senior Leadership

I started my career in February 2006 as a mortgage loan officer. I was 24 years old, fresh out of college, learning the fundamentals of lending, relationship-building, and customer service.

Over the next 19 years, I progressed through multiple roles: mortgage lending, consumer and agricultural lending, commercial ag lending, regional management, and strategic leadership.

In 2021, I became Regional Lending Manager—the first African American in the state of North Carolina within the Farm Credit System to reach this level of leadership since the organization's founding in 1916.

In 2024, I moved into strategic leadership, launching programs that expanded access to capital for underserved communities.

In August 2025, I stepped away to focus on the next chapter, not yet realizing that the passion I had long carried for supporting and equipping leaders would become the very mission behind B.A.T. Positive.

That's the resume. But here's what the resume doesn't tell you:

The sleepless nights. The self-doubt. The mistakes. The conflict. The loneliness. The pressure of being "the first." The weight of knowing that if I failed, it might close doors for others who looked like me.

B.A.T. Positive is what carried me through all of it.

Here's something most people don't understand about leadership: **You can't lead others if you can't lead yourself.**

Before you manage a team, you have to manage you.

Before you set expectations for others, you have to meet expectations for yourself.

Before you hold people accountable, you have to hold yourself accountable.

Self-leadership is the foundation of all leadership.

And self-leadership requires all three pillars of B.A.T.:

Belief: You have to know who you are, what you stand for, and what you won't compromise on.

Action: You have to show up with discipline, consistency, and integrity—even when no one's watching.

Thought: You have to manage your internal dialogue, reframe adversity, and stay focused on what's possible.

Early in my career, I didn't fully understand this. I thought leadership was about managing others. But I learned quickly that **the hardest person you'll ever lead is yourself.**

The Discipline of Self-Leadership

Let me give you an example.

When I decided to pursue my MBA, I was working full-time, supporting my family, and navigating the pressures of a tough economic climate. It would have been easy to quit. To make excuses. To say, "I'll do it later."

But I made a commitment to myself: **I would finish what I started.**

That meant late nights. Sacrificed weekends. Missed opportunities to relax.

But I showed up. Every single day.

That wasn't about leading a team. That was about **leading myself.**

And when I graduated with nearly a 4.0 GPA, I proved something to myself: **I can be trusted to follow through.**

For leaders: If you can't trust yourself to do what you say you'll do, how can you expect your team to trust you?

Self-leadership builds self-trust. And self-trust is the foundation of credibility.

Building Positive Teams

One of the biggest lessons I learned as a Regional Lending Manager was this: **Your team's culture is a reflection of your leadership.**

If your team is negative, look at yourself first.

If your team lacks accountability, ask yourself: *Am I holding myself accountable?*

If your team isn't engaged, ask yourself: *Am I inspiring them? Am I serving them? Am I showing them what's possible?*

When I stepped into leadership, I knew I wanted to build a positive team. I'd been influenced by Jon Gordon's work on building championship cultures, and I wanted to create that same energy with my team.

But I made mistakes early on.

What I Tried That Didn't Work

I tried to force positivity.

I created an incentive program tied to reading Jon Gordon's books. I thought if my team read *The Energy Bus* and *The Power of Positive Leadership*, they'd naturally adopt the principles.

I organized reading groups. I sent motivational messages. I pushed my agenda.

But here's what I didn't do: **I didn't get buy-in first.**

I was so excited about the content that I assumed everyone else would be too. I didn't take time to understand where my team members were. I didn't ask what they needed. I didn't create space for them to own the process.

The result? Some people engaged. But many felt like I was forcing something on them. The energy I wanted to create felt manufactured instead of authentic.

The Turning Point

The turning point came when I shifted my approach.

Instead of pushing a program, I started asking questions:

- *What do you need from me as your leader?*
- *What's working on our team? What's not?*
- *How can we create an environment where everyone thrives?*

I stopped trying to mandate positivity. I started **modeling it.**

I showed up with consistent energy. I served my team. I removed obstacles. I celebrated wins—big and small. I had the hard conversations when needed.

And slowly, the culture shifted.

Not because I forced it. But because I lived it.

When the Culture Finally Clicked

Let me tell you about the moment I knew the culture had shifted.

It was about twenty-four months into my role as Regional Lending Manager. I'd stopped pushing programs and started modeling the behavior I wanted to see.

One afternoon, I got a call from one of my Loan Officers. She said, "Lance, I need to tell you something."

My heart sank. *Here we go. What's the problem?*

But then she said: "One of our team members just had a family emergency and had to leave suddenly. Without being asked, the rest of the team immediately jumped in. They redistributed her workload. They reached out to her customers. They covered for her without complaint."

She continued: "And here's the thing—they didn't do it because they had to. They did it because they wanted to. Because that's who we are now."

That's when I knew: We'd built something real.

This wasn't a forced culture. This wasn't a program. This was a team that genuinely cared about each other and served each other.

Here's what created that shift:

1. I modeled it first.
When team members had personal crises, I adjusted workloads, extended grace, and showed them they mattered more than metrics.

2. I celebrated service publicly.
Every time I saw someone go above and beyond for a teammate, I recognized it in team meetings. Not with rewards—just with acknowledgment.

3. I removed obstacles.
I made it easier for people to help each other by clarifying roles, improving communication, and building systems that supported collaboration.

4. I was consistent.
I showed up the same way every day—win or lose, good news or bad. My team knew what to expect from me.

The result?

We didn't just build a positive culture. We built a *championship* culture.

Our team met and exceeded most of our performance standards. Not because we had the most talent, but because we had the most trust.

For leaders: Culture isn't built through programs. It's built through daily modeling, consistent recognition, and genuine care for your people.

The Principles of Positive Leadership

Here's what I learned about building positive teams:

Principle 1: You set the temperature.
Your team takes emotional cues from you. If you're anxious, they'll be anxious. If you're calm and focused, they'll find stability.

Principle 2: Positivity isn't about ignoring problems.
It's about addressing problems with a solution-focused mindset. It's about saying, "This is hard—and here's how we're going to tackle it together."

Principle 3: Trust is earned through consistency.
You can't just talk about being positive. You have to show up that way every single day—especially when things get hard.

Principle 4: People need to feel valued.
Recognition matters. Encouragement matters. Letting people know they're seen, heard, and appreciated—that matters more than any bonus or incentive.

Principle 5: Serve your team.
Leadership isn't about being served. It's about serving others. When your team knows you care about them—not just their performance—they'll run through walls for you.

The Leadership Crucible: When the Game Was Moving Too Fast

Let me take you to a moment in my leadership journey when everything I believed about myself was tested.

It was 2022. I was a few months into leading my team as Regional Lending Manager.

Our leadership team was participating in a top leadership series facilitated by—let's call him—Dr. Key.

And the game was moving fast.

Too fast.

I felt like I was drowning. I was fielding an endless cycle of questions from my team—from the most basic to the most complicated. On top of that, I was trying to stay on top of all my managerial duties: performance reviews, pipeline management, strategic planning, reporting to senior leadership.

I was stretched thin.

And I wasn't delegating. I wasn't communicating effectively. I wasn't providing clear direction.

Why? Because it's my natural identity to want to help others. I wanted my team members to know they were supported. I wanted to be available. I wanted to solve every problem.

But I realized I couldn't continue at that pace, or burnout was inevitable.

This was also happening as I was attempting to build my identity as a manager. I was trying to figure out who I was as a leader. What my style was. How to balance support with accountability.

It took everything I had during those moments to believe the game would slow down.

To believe my team would eventually become self-sufficient.

To believe they would buy in and want to follow my leadership.

So I leaned into B.A.T.:

Belief: I had to believe I was capable. That I could figure this out. That I was the right person for this role.

Action: I stayed consistent in my messaging. I showed up every day with the same energy. I leaned into branches that were dealing with adversity. I kept the right focus and attitude.

Thought: I fed my mind the right encouragement—sermons, podcasts from Jon Gordon, John Maxwell, Brian Buffini. I sought advice from my peers in other regions. I kept my thoughts on the right track.

But for some reason, the game just didn't slow down.

Until I had a one-on-one coaching session with Dr. Key.

The Breakthrough: Systems and Delegation

Dr. Key quickly identified what I couldn't see: **I had a systems and delegation opportunity.**

He told me, "Lance, you're trying to do everything yourself. You need to create systems to support your leadership. And you need to delegate tasks that don't require your energy or attention."

That was a game-changer.

As soon as I implemented systems and started delegating, the game slowed down. Almost immediately.

Suddenly, I had time. I had bandwidth. I could focus my attention on developing and supporting my team members instead of being a help desk.

I was able to shift my focus to developing the leader in each person.

Because here's the truth: **When you develop the leader in a person, everything around them eventually gets better.**

The Challenge of Delegation

Let me be honest: Delegating was a challenge for me.

And here's why: Years earlier, I had made a decision that I had to be in control of my destiny. I felt that was what it would take for me to reach all of my goals.

I had to do it myself. I had to be in control.

That mindset served me well as an individual contributor. But as a leader? It was holding me back.

One of my mentors had shared a book with me early in my leadership journey—around 2012. It was *What Got You Here Won't Get You There* by Marshall Goldsmith.

At the time, I read it and thought, *This is good.* But I didn't fully grasp it.

It wasn't until years later, when I began leading teams, that the lesson clicked: **The skills that made me successful as an individual contributor wouldn't make me successful as a leader.**

I had to learn the levels of leadership. I had to learn to let go. I had to learn to trust others.

That was an adjustment. But I finally got the lesson.

The Autonomy Lesson

One of the things I shared with my team members early on in my journey as Regional Lending Manager was that I wanted to give them autonomy.

I believed—and still believe—that autonomy is a great way to empower team members without micromanaging them.

If there's one thing I didn't like early in my professional career, it was having a manager hovering over me. I felt distrusted. I knew I could earn anyone's trust, and I wanted to give my team members that same freedom.

So I told each of them in our one-on-ones: "I trust you. I'm giving you autonomy. I'm here to support you, but I'm not going to micromanage you."

But here's what I should have taken into consideration: **Not everybody operates like me.**

Some people need more accountability than others. Some people thrive with autonomy. Others need more structure.

One size does not fit all.

And there will always be employees who take advantage of autonomy. That's just the reality.

So while I still believe in empowering people with autonomy, I learned that it's important to have clear guidelines and procedures in place—regardless of whether you're a leader who values autonomy.

Trust, but verify. Empower, but hold accountable.

Navigating Difficult Employees

Let's be real: **Not every team member will be easy to lead.**

You will inherit people who are disengaged. People who resist change. People who underperform.

And how you handle those situations will define your leadership.

I've dealt with my share of challenging team members. Employees who were consistently late. Employees who didn't meet expectations. Employees who were negative and brought the team down.

Here's what I learned:

Lesson 1: Get curious before you get critical.

When someone underperforms, your first instinct might be frustration. But before you react, ask: *What's really going on here?*

I had a team member once who was missing deadlines and producing subpar work. My initial reaction was frustration—until I had a conversation with him and discovered he was dealing with a personal crisis at home.

That conversation changed everything. We adjusted his workload temporarily. I connected him with resources. And he came back stronger.

If I had reacted from frustration instead of curiosity, I would have lost a good team member.

Lesson 2: Clarity eliminates confusion.

Sometimes people underperform because they genuinely don't understand what's expected of them.

As leaders, we assume people know what we want. But assumptions create gaps.

Be clear. Be specific. And check for understanding.

Lesson 3: Know when to hold and when to fold.

Not every relationship is meant to last.

I've learned that sometimes, the most loving thing you can do is let someone go. Not because they're a bad person, but because they're not the right fit.

I made the mistake early in my leadership of holding on too long to people who weren't aligned with the team's direction. I wanted to "save" them. But in doing so, I hurt the rest of the team.

For leaders: Don't sacrifice the many for the one. If someone consistently doesn't align with the company's values, vision, or standards—and they're unwilling to change—it's time to part ways.

When I Had to Make the Hard Call

Letting go of employees is never a fun thing to do.

A couple of years into my tenure as a lending manager, I had to make the difficult decision of relieving an employee from their responsibilities.

Without getting into specifics, here's what I learned from that experience:

It's easy to focus our attention on the negative impact of the situation. And no manager wants to do that.

But as leaders, we must realize that sometimes we're actually *helping* that person get closer to their purpose by parting ways.

It's a two-way street.

As a leader, it's our responsibility to ensure our team members have all the tools to be successful. We can enhance skills. We can provide training, coaching, resources, and support.

But here's what we *can't* teach: **will.**

When the will isn't there—when someone isn't aligned with the mission, isn't committed to growth, or isn't willing to meet the standards—it's our responsibility as leaders to make the appropriate decision.

A decision that upholds our core values.

A decision that protects the positive culture we've built.

A decision that serves the organization and the rest of the team.

After you've tried everything you can as a leader, it's okay to recognize that making the tough decision is often the best decision.

Not just for the organization.

Not just for the team.

But for the person themselves—because staying in a role where they're not thriving isn't serving them either.

Here's what I tell leaders facing this situation:

1. Do the work first.
Make sure you've provided clear expectations, coaching, feedback, and resources. Document everything. Give them every opportunity to succeed.

2. Make the decision with compassion.
This isn't about punishment. It's about alignment. You can let someone go with dignity and respect.

3. Communicate clearly and directly.
Don't drag it out. Don't sugarcoat it. Be honest, be kind, and be clear.

4. Protect the rest of your team.
Your team is watching. When you tolerate underperformance or misalignment, you send a message that standards don't matter. That erodes trust and morale.

5. Give yourself grace.
These decisions are hard. You'll second-guess yourself. That's normal. But if you've done the work, trust your judgment.

The hardest decisions are often the right decisions.

And sometimes, the most loving thing you can do—for your team, your organization, and even the person you're letting go—is to make the call.

The Lonely Road of Leadership

Let me tell you something nobody prepares you for: **Leadership is lonely.**

The higher you climb, the fewer people you can confide in.

The decisions you make affect people's livelihoods, and that weight sits on your shoulders alone.

You're expected to have the answers—even when you don't.

You're expected to stay strong—even when you're struggling.

And sometimes, the loneliest part of leadership is being the only one who looks like you in the room.

When I became a Regional Lending Manager in 2021, I didn't have a next-level model who looked like me. I was the first African American in North Carolina within the Farm Credit System to reach that level since 1916.

That was an honor. But it was also a weight.

Every decision felt magnified. Every mistake felt like it could reinforce a narrative I didn't want to perpetuate.

There were nights I questioned everything.

Am I good enough? Am I the right person for this? What if I fail?

But then I remembered: **Cycles repeat until someone breaks them.**

I could either let the weight crush me, or I could carry it with purpose.

I chose purpose.

How to Lead Through Loneliness

Here's what helped me navigate the lonely road:

1. Anchor yourself in your "why."
When leadership gets hard, your purpose is what keeps you going. I knew my "why"—to break cycles, to create opportunities for others, to prove that your zip code doesn't determine your destiny.

2. Find trusted advisors outside your organization.
You can't always confide in people you lead. But you need people you can

be vulnerable with. Find mentors, peers, or coaches who can speak into your life.

3. Remember: You're not alone, even when it feels that way.

God has been my anchor. Faith has sustained me when everything else felt shaky.

4. Give yourself grace.

You won't get it right every time. You'll make mistakes. You'll have bad days. That's okay. You're human.

Leading Through Change and Adversity

One of the hardest seasons of my leadership was managing a team through high turnover, challenging market conditions, and organizational change.

People were frustrated. Morale was low. And I was under pressure from senior leadership to deliver results we weren't fully resourced to achieve.

I questioned everything.

Am I the right leader for this? Am I doing more harm than good?

But I kept coming back to the B.A.T. framework:

Belief: I believed in the mission. I believed in my team. I believed that we could get through this together.

Action: I showed up every day. I had the hard conversations. I served my team even when I was exhausted.

Thought: I chose to focus on what was possible, not what was broken. I anchored my team in hope, not despair.

And we made it through.

Not perfectly. Not without scars. But we made it.

For leaders: Change is inevitable. Adversity is guaranteed. Your job isn't to eliminate the hard seasons—it's to lead your team through them.

Training Your Replacement: A Leadership Philosophy

Let me share something about my leadership philosophy that might surprise you:

I train people to replace me.

That's right. My goal as a leader is to develop people who can step into my role—and do it even better than I did.

Some leaders hoard knowledge. They keep their secrets close. They're threatened by talented people on their team.

Not me.

I believe that if I'm not raising up leaders who can replace me, I'm not really leading—I'm just managing.

I also try to encourage leaders within my team to do the same. It's part of lifting others so that they can grow and meet their fullest potential in their given role or to meet their development objectives.

It's important to note that not everyone subscribes to this form of leadership.

Here's why this matters:

When you train people to replace you, you:

- Free yourself to move to the next level
- Build a pipeline of ready leaders
- Create a culture of growth and development
- Prove that you care more about the mission than your own position

And here's the beautiful irony: **The more you train people to replace you, the more valuable you become.**

Because organizations don't promote people who can't be replaced. They promote people who have built systems and developed leaders so strong that the organization can thrive without them.

For leaders: Are you training your replacement? Are you developing people who can step into your role?

If not, you're limiting your own growth—and theirs.

If I could go back and give my younger leadership self advice, here's what I'd say:

1. You don't have to have all the answers.

What I wish I'd known: It's okay to say, "I don't know, but I'll find out." Vulnerability builds trust.

What I learned: I used to think leaders had to know everything. But the best leaders I've encountered are the ones who admit when they don't know—and then go find the answer. That honesty creates psychological safety for your team.

2. Balance the scale.

What I wish I'd known: I leaned too heavily toward encouragement and support, and not enough toward accountability.

What I learned: I once kept an underperforming team member on too long because I wanted to "save" them. My team knew it. And my credibility suffered. I learned that compassion without accountability isn't kindness— it's enabling. Great leaders do both.

3. Not everyone is coachable.

What I wish I'd known: You can't force growth on someone who doesn't want it.

What I learned: I spent months trying to develop someone who wasn't interested in growing. I poured energy, time, and resources into them—

energy I could have invested in hungry team members. Save your energy for the people who want it.

4. Protect your mental and physical health.

What I wish I'd known: Leadership is a marathon, not a sprint. If you burn out, you can't lead anyone.

What I learned: I pushed through exhaustion, stress, and warning signs that my body was breaking down. I thought powering through was strength. It wasn't—it was foolishness. You can't pour from an empty cup.

5. Delegation isn't weakness–it's multiplication.

What I wish I'd known: Trying to do everything yourself limits your impact.

What I learned: Marshall Goldsmith was right: What got you here won't get you there. I had to let go of control and trust my team. When I finally did, my impact multiplied.

6. Your legacy isn't your title–it's the people you raise up.

What I wish I'd known: The greatest measure of your leadership is who you develop, not what you accomplish.

What I learned: Years from now, nobody will remember my portfolio size or my production numbers. But they'll remember if I believed in them, invested in them, and helped them become better leaders. That's legacy.

Before you move to the final chapter, take a moment to reflect:

1. **Are you leading yourself before you try to lead others?** What's one area of self-leadership you need to strengthen?
2. **What cycle are you perpetuating in your organization or team?** How can you be a cycle-breaker?
3. **Who are you raising up?** Who are you investing in that doesn't benefit you directly?

Action Challenges

1. **Identify one person on your team who needs encouragement—and give it to them this week.** Be specific about what you see in them.
2. **Assess your leadership balance.** Are you leaning too heavily toward support or accountability? Commit to bringing more balance this month.
3. **Find a trusted advisor outside your organization.** Someone you can be vulnerable with. Schedule a conversation with them this week.

Leadership is hard.

But it's also the most rewarding work you'll ever do.

When you lead with B.A.T. Positive—when you anchor yourself in belief, show up with consistent action, and master your mindset—you don't just survive leadership. You thrive in it.

And you create space for others to thrive too.

Now let's talk about your legacy.

PART 4: LEGACY

CHAPTER 7

The Become It: Your Turn to Lead

We've come a long way together.

You've walked with me through the projects of Spartanburg. You've met Aunt Bob and learned the philosophy that shaped my life. You've seen how B.A.T. Positive carried me from entry-level loan officer to senior leadership.

But here's the truth: **This book was never just about my story.**

It was about giving you a framework—a proven, practical, life-changing framework—that you can use to transform your own leadership, your own life, and the lives of the people you influence.

This final chapter is about you.

It's about how you apply B.A.T. Positive in every area of your life. It's about the legacy you're building. It's about the cycles you're breaking and the doors you're opening for others.

Because leadership isn't just about what you accomplish. It's about who you raise up.

Let's talk about your legacy.

B.A.T. Positive isn't just a leadership framework. **It's a life framework.**

It works in your career, yes. But it also works in your marriage, your parenting, your friendships, your community involvement, and your personal growth.

Let me show you how.

B.A.T. as a Parent

As a father of three, I've learned that parenting is one of the hardest—and most important—leadership roles you'll ever have.

And B.A.T. applies here too.

Belief: Your children are watching what you believe about yourself, about them, and about the world. If you believe they're capable, they'll start to believe it too. If you believe in discipline and structure, they'll internalize those values.

Action: Your kids won't remember everything you say. But they'll remember what you do. Do you show up for them? Do you keep your promises? Do you model the character you're trying to instill?

Thought: How you think about parenting shapes how you parent. If you see every tantrum as a battle, you'll parent from frustration. If you see every challenge as a teaching moment, you'll parent from wisdom.

For parents: Be intentional. Model B.A.T. for your kids. They're learning from you every single day—whether you realize it or not.

B.A.T. as a Spouse

Marriage requires the same framework.

Belief: Do you believe in your spouse? Do you believe in your marriage? Your belief will determine how you show up in the relationship.

Action: Love is a verb. It's not just a feeling—it's a daily decision to serve, to sacrifice, to show up even when it's hard.

Thought: How you think about your spouse matters. If you focus on their flaws, that's all you'll see. If you focus on their strengths, you'll build them up.

For spouses: B.A.T. keeps marriages strong. Believe in each other. Act with love and intentionality. Think the best of each other.

B.A.T. as a Friend

Friendship is leadership too.

Belief: Believe in your friends. See their potential. Speak life into them.

Action: Show up. Be present. Invest time and energy into the relationships that matter.

Thought: How you think about your friendships will determine the quality of those friendships. Choose to see the good.

B.A.T. as a Community Leader

Whether you're leading in your church, your neighborhood, or a nonprofit organization, B.A.T. applies.

Belief: Believe in the mission. Believe in the people you're serving. Believe that change is possible.

Action: Don't just talk about making a difference—do it. Show up. Serve. Sacrifice.

Thought: Think long-term. Think impact. Think legacy.

Bringing B.A.T. to Your Organization

Now let's talk about how to bring B.A.T. Positive into your organization.

Whether you're a team leader, a department head, or a senior executive, you have the power to shape culture. And B.A.T. Positive is a tool you can use to do it.

Step 1: Model It First

You can't teach what you don't live.

Before you introduce B.A.T. to your team, you have to embody it yourself.

Are you anchored in belief?

Are you taking consistent action?

Are you managing your mindset?

Your team will follow what you do, not just what you say.

Step 2: Teach the Framework

Once you're living it, introduce it to your team.

You can do this through:

- Team meetings
- One-on-one coaching sessions
- Training workshops
- Book studies (yes, this book!)

Explain the three pillars:

- **Belief:** Who we are, what we stand for, our values
- **Action:** What we do every day, our consistency, our discipline
- **Thought:** How we think, how we manage our mindset, how we see challenges

Make it simple. Make it memorable. Make it actionable.

Step 3: Reinforce It Daily

Culture isn't built in a day. It's built through daily reinforcement.

Ask yourself:

- *How can I remind my team of B.A.T. every day?*
- *How can I recognize people who exemplify it?*
- *How can I address behaviors that contradict it?*

Consistency is key.

Step 4: Create Systems Around It

B.A.T. should be woven into how you operate.

For example:

Belief: Make your values visible. Put them on the wall. Reference them in meetings. Hire based on alignment with them.

Action: Set clear expectations. Track consistency. Celebrate discipline.

Thought: Create space for reflection. Encourage gratitude. Address negativity quickly.

When B.A.T. becomes part of your systems, it becomes part of your culture.

Navigating Transitions: When Life Demands You Pivot

Let's talk about something every leader faces but few people prepare you for: **transitions.**

Life doesn't move in straight lines. You'll face moments when everything changes—moments that demand you pivot, adapt, and recalibrate.

Transitions come in many forms:

- Career changes (layoffs, promotions, new industries, entrepreneurship)
- Life changes (marriage, divorce, parenthood, loss of a loved one)
- Identity changes (from individual contributor to leader, from employee to executive, from professional to retiree)

And here's the truth: **Transitions are disorienting.**

Even good transitions—promotions, new opportunities, exciting changes—can throw you off balance. Because transitions force you to let go of what was familiar and step into the unknown.

But B.A.T. is your anchor in transitions.

Let me show you how.

Belief: When Everything Changes, Your Values Stay Constant

In a transition, the first thing you lose is certainty. You don't know what the new normal will look like. You don't know if you're making the right decision. You don't know how things will turn out.

But here's what doesn't change: **who you are.**

Your core values. Your character. Your "why." Those are constants.

In transition, anchor back to belief:

Ask yourself:

- *Who am I, regardless of my title or my circumstances?*
- *What do I stand for, no matter what's changing around me?*
- *What's my "why"—and does this transition align with it?*

When everything around you is shifting, your belief system is the foundation that holds you steady.

Action: Take One Small Step

Transitions are overwhelming because they demand so much change at once. You feel paralyzed because you don't have the whole plan figured out.

But here's the secret: **You don't need the whole plan. You just need the next step.**

In transition, focus on small, intentional actions:

1. Acknowledge the disruption.
Don't pretend it's not happening. Don't minimize it. Say out loud: "This is a transition. It's hard. And that's okay."

2. Identify one action you can take today.
What's the one thing you can do right now that moves you forward? Do that. Just that.

3. Build momentum through micro-wins.
Every small action you take in the right direction creates momentum. And momentum carries you through uncertainty.

Remember: You don't conquer transitions in one day. You navigate them one step at a time.

Thought: Reframe the Transition as Opportunity

Finally, you have to manage your mindset.

Transitions trigger fear. Fear of the unknown. Fear of failure. Fear of loss.

But the way you think about the transition determines how you experience it.

Here's the reframe:

Instead of: *"Everything is falling apart."*
Choose: *"Everything is being rearranged for something better."*

Instead of: *"I don't know what I'm doing."*
Choose: *"I'm learning. Growth happens in the unknown."*

Instead of: *"This is happening TO me."*
Choose: *"This is happening FOR me. What is this transition trying to teach me?"*

Ask yourself:
"What's the opportunity here that I'm not seeing yet?"

Putting It All Together: B.A.T. in Transition

Without B.A.T.:
You spiral. You panic. You make impulsive decisions or freeze in indecision. You lose sight of who you are. You let fear drive your choices.

With B.A.T.:
You anchor in your belief system. You take one small step. You reframe the transition as an opportunity for growth.

And months later, you look back and realize: that transition was a turning point. It refined you. It prepared you. It positioned you for what's next.

Transitions are inevitable. But with B.A.T., they become opportunities for growth, not reasons to quit.

Breaking Cycles: The Competitive Advantage

Let me bring us back to something we've talked about throughout this book: **cycles.**

Cycles repeat until someone breaks them.

In families. In communities. In organizations. In industries.

And you have the power to be a cycle-breaker.

But here's what I want you to understand: **Breaking cycles isn't just the right thing to do. It's a competitive advantage.**

1. Diversity of Thought Drives Innovation

Research from McKinsey shows that companies in the top quartile for ethnic and cultural diversity outperform those in the bottom quartile by 36% in profitability.

Why?

Because when you break cycles—when you open doors for people who don't fit the traditional mold—you bring in fresh perspectives, new ideas, and creative problem-solving.

Homogeneous teams think alike. Diverse teams innovate.

Breaking the cycle of "we've always hired people like us" creates a competitive edge.

2. Breaking Toxic Cycles Reduces Turnover

Gallup research shows that 75% of employees who voluntarily leave their jobs do so because of their direct manager—not the company.

Think about that.

Three out of four people who quit aren't quitting the job. They're quitting the leadership.

When leaders break cycles of poor leadership—when they choose to lead differently than they were led—they create cultures where people want to stay.

And retention saves money. The cost of replacing an employee ranges from 50-200% of their annual salary, depending on the role.

Cycle-breaking isn't just the right thing to do. It's financially smart.

3. Inclusive Leadership Expands Talent Pools

When organizations break cycles of who "traditionally" gets opportunities, they expand their talent pool exponentially.

Deloitte research found that inclusive teams make better business decisions 87% of the time, and they make those decisions twice as fast.

Why?

Because inclusive leaders tap into talent others overlook. They don't limit themselves to people who look like them, think like them, or come from the same background.

Breaking the cycle of exclusion creates access to untapped potential.

4. Cycle-Breakers Build Legacy Organizations

Organizations that break cycles don't just survive—they thrive across generations.

Think about companies known for developing leaders: General Electric under Jack Welch. Procter & Gamble. McKinsey.

What do they have in common?

They intentionally broke the cycle of "hoarding talent" and instead built systems to develop and deploy leaders.

That's how you build a legacy organization—not by keeping people in place, but by preparing them to rise.

So Here's the Question for You as a Leader:

What cycle are you perpetuating?

Is it a cycle of:

- Only promoting people who look like the current leadership?
- Toxic management styles passed down from generation to generation?
- Risk-averse decision-making that stifles innovation?
- Treating employees as replaceable instead of developable?

And more importantly: **Are you willing to be the leader who breaks it?**

Because when you break unhealthy cycles, you don't just change your team. You change your organization. And you create space for others to do the same.

Opening Doors: The Responsibility of Leadership

Here's a truth about leadership that not enough people talk about:

Every door you walk through, you have a responsibility to hold open for others.

Not just for people who look like you. Not just for people who remind you of yourself.

For anyone with hunger, character, and potential.

The Principle: Leaders Create Leaders

Average leaders hoard opportunity. They see talented people as threats.

Great leaders multiply opportunity. They see talented people as investments.

When you open doors for others, you:

- Expand the leadership pipeline
- Build trust and loyalty
- Create a reputation as a developer of people
- Ensure the organization thrives beyond your tenure

This is what separates managers from leaders.

Managers protect their position. Leaders prepare their replacement.

The Practice: How to Open Doors

Opening doors isn't passive. It's intentional. Here's how you do it:

1. Advocate for people who aren't in the room.

When promotion discussions happen, who are you championing?

Are you only advocating for people who look like you, think like you, or remind you of yourself?

Or are you willing to advocate for the overlooked, the underestimated, the different?

Your voice in closed-door conversations can change someone's trajectory.

2. Share knowledge generously.

Don't hoard what you know. Teach it. Share it. Give it away.

The more you empower others with knowledge, the more valuable you become—because you're known as someone who builds, not someone who protects.

Knowledge shared is knowledge multiplied.

3. Create opportunities intentionally.

Who are you giving stretch assignments to?

Who are you inviting into rooms they've never been in?

Who are you exposing to leaders they need to know?

Opportunity isn't just about promoting people. It's about positioning them for growth.

4. Give credit publicly.

When your team succeeds, make sure they get the recognition—not you.

Leaders who share credit build loyalty. Leaders who take credit build resentment.

Your job is to shine the spotlight on others, not yourself.

The Power of Relationships and Mentorship

Here's something I need you to understand: **No one gets there alone.**

Relationships are essential. Partnerships are critical.

There's a quote I've held onto for years—I believe it's from Jim Rohn: **"Relationships are the linchpin to success."**

And it's true.

But here's what's equally important: **Not all relationships are created equal.**

You can be in good relationships that propel you forward. Or you can be in unhealthy relationships that hold you back.

The key is **reciprocity.**

You want to be in relationships where both parties are adding value to one another—where it's **give-give, not give-take.**

When you have strong relationships and meaningful partnerships, you can go far. You can have real impact.

And here's what I've found: When you have strong, positive relationships, problems don't seem as big—because you have someone to weather the storms with you.

The Mentor Who Changed My Leadership Journey

I have many relationships. And let me tell you, I had to lean on those relationships during my leadership journey.

I like to surround myself with leaders and forward thinkers. There's this inquisitive part of me that always wants to know what makes great CEOs tick. What separates good leaders from exceptional ones.

I've been fortunate enough to call a few CEOs my friends.

But there was one particular CEO who supported me during the growing pains as a Regional Lending Manager. Someone who saw something in me before I fully saw it in myself.

I met him in 2019. He'd recently retired, and he was in his late 70s. Not only did he bring decades of leadership experience—he also brought a deep well of wisdom.

He took me under his wing.

We had countless conversations. He shared perspectives I'd never considered. He gave me wisdom I couldn't have gained anywhere else. And he gave me something even more valuable: **access.**

He told me I could call him anytime. Day or night. He wanted me to know that I didn't have to walk the leadership journey alone.

And that changed everything.

When I was drowning in the early months of regional leadership—when the game was moving too fast and I questioned whether I belonged—he was the one I called.

When I faced decisions I'd never faced before, he walked me through them.

When I doubted myself, he reminded me of what he saw in me.

He didn't just give me knowledge. He gave me perspective, wisdom, and belief.

And that's what the right mentor does.

Why Every Leader Needs a Mentor

Here's what I want you to understand, especially if you're an emerging leader:

You are intelligent.

You are gifted.

You are skilled.

You've been successful.

But you also have **blind spots.**

You have experiences you've never encountered. Challenges you've never faced. Decisions you've never had to make.

And wisdom from a respected leader can close that gap.

A great mentor:

- Sees what you can't see
- Challenges your thinking
- Shares lessons from their own failures
- Opens doors you didn't know existed
- Gives you access to a larger network of thought leaders

But here's the key: **You have to find the RIGHT mentor for you.**

Not just anyone with a title. Not just someone successful.

The right mentor.

How to Identify the Right Mentor: The B.A.T. Framework

So how do you identify the right mentor? Use the B.A.T. framework:

Belief: Do They Believe in You?

The right mentor sees something in you that you might not fully see in yourself yet.

They don't just tolerate you—they **invest** in you.

They believe you're capable of more. They challenge you to think bigger. They push you toward your potential.

Ask yourself:

- *Does this person genuinely believe in my potential?*
- *Do they see me as someone worth investing in?*
- *Do they speak life into me, or just give advice?*

If a mentor doesn't believe in you, the relationship won't work. Mentorship requires belief.

Action: Are They Willing to Invest Time and Energy?

The right mentor doesn't just talk—they act.

They make themselves available. They show up. They invest time, energy, and access.

Look for these signs:

- They give you their time—not just once, but consistently
- They open doors for you (introductions, opportunities, networks)
- They check in on you, even when you're not asking for help
- They're willing to have the hard conversations, not just the easy ones

Ask yourself:

- *Is this person willing to invest in me, or are they just being polite?*
- *Do they follow through on what they say they'll do?*
- *Are they accessible, or am I just another name on their list?*

If someone says they want to mentor you but never makes time, they're not the right mentor.

Thought: Do They Challenge Your Thinking?

The right mentor doesn't just affirm you—they **stretch** you.

They challenge your assumptions. They ask hard questions. They make you think differently.

A great mentor doesn't just give you answers—they help you discover better questions.

Look for these signs:

- They ask questions that make you think deeper
- They challenge your blind spots
- They push back on your ideas (respectfully) to make them stronger
- They share perspectives you wouldn't have considered on your own

Ask yourself:

- *Does this person make me think differently?*
- *Do they challenge me to grow, or just validate where I am?*
- *Do I leave conversations with them feeling stretched, not just comfortable?*

If a mentor only tells you what you want to hear, they're not helping you grow.

How to Approach a Potential Mentor

So you've identified someone you'd like to learn from. Now what?

Here's how to approach them:

1. Be specific about what you're asking for.

Don't just say, "Will you mentor me?"

Say: "I'm navigating [specific challenge]. I admire how you've [specific accomplishment]. Would you be willing to meet with me quarterly to share your perspective?"

2. Respect their time.

Don't ask for open-ended, ongoing commitments. Start small. Ask for one conversation. Prove you're coachable. Then build from there.

3. Come prepared.

Don't waste their time. Show up with specific questions. Take notes. Apply what they share. And follow up to let them know the impact of their guidance.

4. **Give before you ask.**

How can you add value to them? Can you share an article they'd find helpful? Introduce them to someone in your network? Offer to help with something they're working on?

Mentorship is give-give, not give-take. Start by giving.

What Mentorship Gave Me

Looking back, that CEO who mentored me gave me far more than knowledge.

He gave me:

- **Confidence** when I doubted myself
- **Perspective** when I was too close to a problem
- **Wisdom** from mistakes I didn't have to make myself
- **Access** to a network of leaders I never would have reached on my own
- **Belief** that I belonged in the room, even when I felt like an imposter

And that made my leadership journey not just bearable—it made it meaningful.

Your Turn

So here's my challenge to you:

Who's one leader you can reach out to this month?

Not someone famous. Not someone untouchable.

Someone who's 5-10 years ahead of you. Someone who's walked a path you're trying to walk. Someone who might be willing to invest in you.

Reach out. Be specific. Be respectful. And see what happens.

Because the right mentor can change the trajectory of your leadership—and your life.

The Ripple Effect: Legacy Leadership

Here's the beautiful thing about opening doors:

When you open doors for one person, they open doors for others.

And that creates a ripple effect that extends far beyond your direct influence.

Think about the leaders who opened doors for you.

Maybe it was a mentor who saw potential in you. A boss who gave you a shot when others wouldn't. A teacher who believed in you when you didn't believe in yourself.

Now think about the people YOU'RE opening doors for.

And imagine them doing the same for others.

That's how movements start.

That's how cultures change.

That's how legacies are built.

The Power Box Promise: Full Circle

Let me take you back to where we started.

There's a green power box behind a playground in the Ellen C. Watson apartments on the west side of Spartanburg, South Carolina.

When I was thirteen years old, I sat next to that power box and made a promise to myself:

I'm going to be successful.

I'm going to prove them all wrong.

Nobody will ever make me feel this way again.

That promise changed my life.

But here's what I've learned since then:

The promise wasn't just about me.

It was about every kid who grows up feeling unwanted.

Every person who's told they're not good enough.

Every leader who's the first to walk through a door.

Every dream that seems impossible.

The promise was about breaking cycles and opening doors.

And now, decades later, I can look back and say:

I kept the promise.

Not perfectly. Not without struggle. But I kept it.

And now I'm passing the baton to you.

Your Power Box Moment

So here's my question for you:

What's your power box moment?

What's the moment when you made a promise to yourself—or when you need to make one?

What's the vow that will change the trajectory of your life?

Don't wait for the perfect moment. Don't wait until you have it all figured out.

Make the promise now.

Write it down. Speak it out loud. Commit to it.

And then let B.A.T. Positive be the framework that helps you keep it.

Your Legacy Starts Now

Legacy isn't something you think about at the end of your life.

Legacy is what you're building right now.

With every decision you make.

With every person you invest in.

With every cycle you break.

With every door you open.

Your legacy is being written today.

So the question is: **What do you want it to say?**

Do you want people to say you were talented? Or that you were a developer of talent?

Do you want people to say you were successful? Or that you made others successful?

Do you want people to say you had a good career? Or that you changed lives?

The choice is yours.

The Final Charge

If you take nothing else from this book, take this:

Believe in yourself. You are more capable than you think. Your past does not define your future. Your circumstances do not dictate your destiny.

Act with intention. Stop waiting. Stop making excuses. Pick up the bat and swing. Consistent action, over time, creates extraordinary results.

Think positively. Master your mindset. Reframe failure. See opportunity in adversity. Be a dealer of hope.

And lead with B.A.T. Positive.

Because when you align your belief, your action, and your thought—you don't just survive. You thrive.

And you create space for others to thrive too.

Over thirty years ago, I sat next to a green power box behind the Ellen C. Watson apartments in Spartanburg, South Carolina.

I was thirteen years old. Both parents had rejected me. I felt unwanted, overlooked, forgotten.

And in that moment, I made a promise to myself:

I'm going to be successful. I'm going to prove them all wrong. Nobody will ever make me feel this way again.

That promise changed everything.

But it wasn't just the promise that carried me through. It was what Aunt Bob taught me every single day after that moment.

She looked at a broken kid from the projects and said:

"Be positive. Act positive. Think positive. And positive things will happen to you and for you."

She believed in me when I didn't believe in myself.

She saw potential in me that I couldn't see.

She planted a seed that would grow for decades.

And it changed everything.

Now it's your turn.

Find your power box moment. That defining decision. That promise you need to make to yourself.

It might not be next to an actual power box. It might be in your office, your car, your living room, or a quiet moment alone.

But it's there. Waiting for you.

What promise will you make?

What legacy will you build?

And once you've made that promise, I want you to do what Aunt Bob taught me:

Be positive. Act positive. Think positive.

Plant seeds in others.

Believe in someone who doesn't believe in themselves.

See potential others can't see.

Be a dealer of hope.

Because twenty years from now, someone will look back and say:

"You changed my life."

And that, my friend, is legacy.

Your situation does not dictate your destination.

Your past does not define your future.

Your circumstances do not determine your destiny.

You do.

With belief. With action. With thought.

Now go. Lead. Thrive.

Find your power box moment.

Make your promise.

And never let go.

Before you close this book, take a moment to reflect:

1. **What's your power box moment?** What promise do you need to make to yourself today?
2. **Who are you raising up?** Who needs you to be a dealer of hope for them?
3. **What will your legacy say?** What do you want to be remembered for?

Action Challenges

1. **Make your power box promise.** Write it down. Speak it out loud. Commit to it.
2. **Identify one person you're going to invest in this month.** Someone who needs you to believe in them, train them, or open a door for them.
3. **Share this book.** If B.A.T. Positive has impacted you, pass it on. Give it to a colleague, a friend, a family member. Plant the seed in someone else's life.

CONTINUE THE JOURNEY

Ready to go deeper with The Power Box Framework?

TAKE THE POWER BOX ASSESSMENT

Discover your strengths in Belief, Action, and Thought—and get a personalized development plan.

Visit: www.batpositive.com

Access the B.A.T. Leadership Development Tools

Access the Leadership Assessment, reflection guides, and action plan templates designed to help you apply the B.A.T. Framework with clarity and intention. These development tools are crafted to support your growth, strengthen self-awareness, and help you take meaningful action as a leader.

ABOUT THE AUTHOR

Lance Wardlaw is a speaker, author, and coach specializing in agriculture finance and leadership, dedicated to helping leaders become the best version of themselves and live their life's purpose through the B.A.T. Positive framework.

For nearly two decades, Lance served in agricultural finance with Farm Credit. He led teams, managed key client relationships across the region, and as Director of Strategic Alliances, built the AgStrong program for AgSouth Farm Credit—expanding access to capital for underserved communities. His journey from the housing projects of Spartanburg, South Carolina, to senior leadership is a testament to the power of belief, action, and mindset.

In August 2025, Lance stepped away from his senior leadership role to focus fully on his mission: equipping leaders to unlock their potential and lead with impact.

Lance holds an MBA from Capella University and a Bachelor's degree in Finance/Banking from East Tennessee State University. He is the author of *What About Me? Words of Advice to Help Young People Navigate Challenges, Seize Opportunities and Make Better Choices.*

He lives in Winston-Salem, North Carolina, with his wife, Selena, and their three children: Marina, Landon, and Harrison.

Connect with Lance:

- Website: www.batpositive.com
- LinkedIn: linkedin.com/in/lance-wardlaw-mba-5a153054
- Speaking & Consulting: batpositive@gmail.com

ACKNOWLEDGMENTS

This book would not exist without the people who invested in me, believed in me, and refused to let me settle for less than what I was capable of.

To my wife and children: Thank you for your patience, your support, and your love. You are my "why." Everything I do is to create a better future for you and to model what it means to lead with integrity.

To Aunt Bob (Bobbie Higgins): You saved my life. You gave me structure, faith, and a philosophy that has carried me through every challenge. "Be positive, act positive, think positive"—those words shaped everything I am. Thank you for breaking the cycle and showing me a different way.

To my brother, Lester Wardlaw: You have always been my hero and my first in-person model. Your positive attitude, your willingness to take risks, and your example showed me what was possible. You helped me believe so much was within reach, challenged me to think beyond my current circumstances, and paved the way for me to follow in your footsteps. Thank you for setting the bar high and for always being there when I needed you.

To my mother: Your strength—even in your hardest moments—showed me resilience. Thank you for your love, wisdom, and the lessons that shaped who I am today.

To Coach Smiley (in loving memory): You saw potential in me when I was just a kid trying to figure out who I was. You believed in me when I didn't believe in myself. You pushed me to be better, to work harder, to never settle. Though you are no longer with us, your impact on my life remains. Thank you for planting seeds that would grow for decades. I honor your memory and carry your lessons with me always.

To the many leaders who played a significant role in my development: Your investment in me made all the difference. Thank you for seeing potential, opening doors, and challenging me to grow.

To my peers, mentors, and colleagues in the Farm Credit System: Thank you for the exposure, the opportunities, and the development. This organization supported my journey, and I'm forever grateful.

To every team member I've had the privilege to lead: Thank you for trusting me, challenging me, and making me better. Even in the hard moments, you taught me what leadership really means.

To my family—my brothers, my cousins, my extended family: We made it. We broke the cycle. This is for all of us.

To the reader: I hope this book encourages and strengthens you on your journey of self-discovery. Embrace your flaws and strengths, and know that your story is extraordinary. Pursue your best self with confidence.

Finally, to God: Thank You for Your grace, Your purpose, Your protection, and Your peace. Thank You for the reminder that I can do all things through Christ who strengthens me.

NOTES

Chapter 3: Be Positive (Belief)

- Proverbs 23:7 (KJV): "For as he thinketh in his heart, so is he."
- Philippians 4:13 (KJV): "I can do all things through Christ which strengtheneth me."
- Values-based leadership research: Studies show that leaders anchored in clear values make more consistent decisions and build higher-trust cultures.

Chapter 4: Act Positive (Action)

- Compound effect principle: Based on Darren Hardy's *The Compound Effect* (2010), which demonstrates how small, consistent actions create exponential results over time.
- Service and sacrifice research: Studies on servant leadership show that leaders who prioritize service create more engaged, loyal teams.

Chapter 5: Think Positive (Mindset)

- Daniel Goleman, *Emotional Intelligence: Why It Can Matter More Than IQ* (1995): Research showing that EQ accounts for nearly 90% of what sets high performers apart from peers with similar technical skills.
- Viktor Frankl, *Man's Search for Meaning* (1946): "Between stimulus and response there is a space. In that space is our power to choose our response."

- Neuroscience of mindset: Research shows that the brain reinforces patterns of thought—positive or negative—based on what we consistently focus on.
- Reticular Activating System (RAS): The brain's filtering mechanism that determines what information reaches conscious awareness, programmable through focused attention.
- Gratitude research: Studies show that regular gratitude practice reduces stress and depression, improves sleep, strengthens immune function, and increases life satisfaction.

Chapter 6: B.A.T. in Leadership

- Marshall Goldsmith, *What Got You Here Won't Get You There* (2007): Explores how the skills that make individual contributors successful often don't translate to leadership roles.

Chapter 7: The B.A.T. Legacy

- Jim Rohn: "Relationships are the linchpin to success."
- McKinsey & Company (2020): Companies in the top quartile for ethnic and cultural diversity outperform those in the bottom quartile by 36% in profitability.
- Gallup Research: 75% of employees who voluntarily leave their jobs do so because of their direct manager.
- Deloitte Research: Inclusive teams make better business decisions 87% of the time and make those decisions twice as fast.

RECOMMENDED READING

For readers who want to go deeper into the themes explored in *B.A.T. Positive*, here are some books that have influenced my journey:

- *Emotional Intelligence* by Daniel Goleman
- *Man's Search for Meaning* by Viktor Frankl
- *What Got You Here Won't Get You There* by Marshall Goldsmith
- *The Energy Bus* by Jon Gordon
- *The Power of Positive Leadership* by Jon Gordon
- *Start With Why* by Simon Sinek
- *Good to Great* by Jim Collins
- *The 5 Levels of Leadership* by John Maxwell
- *The Compound Effect* by Darren Hardy
- *Dare to Lead* by Brené Brown
- *Mindset: The New Psychology of Success* by Carol S. Dweck

www.ingramcontent.com/pod-product-compliance
Lightning Source LLC
Chambersburg PA
CBHW071746150726
47998CB00005B/1832